Wings for Change

Systemic organizational development

Wings for Change – *Systemic organizational development*

Jan-Jacob Stam

Originally published under title: Vleugels voor verandering

© 2017, Systemic Books Publishing

ISBN 978-94-92331-08-3 (NUR 801)

Contents

Preface

This is a book about organisations. About organisations seen from a systemic perspective. There are many ways of looking at organisations and this is simply one of them. Some might find this perspective a little strange; just see what pleases you in it and what does not. Maybe there are eye openers; maybe it will touch you or maybe you will not like it at all.

Systemic work's full name is systemic phenomenological work. It is a branch on the tree of system-approaches applied to organisations. By phenomenological we mean that we see and accept reality exactly as it is revealed to us.

The systemic way of looking is an approach, a philosophy and a different way of looking at the world. It provides a complementary and sometimes surprising image of reality.

Another branch of this systemic tree is a method we can easily use to examine reality. Known as a constellation, it was developed in Germany, with Bert Hellinger making the most important contribution. Family constellations are now rather well known in the Netherlands and many other countries around the world; organisational constellations are also becoming an increasingly well-known and trusted tool, especially among organisational consultants. Trusted, even though, as yet, we do not know how a constellation actually works. When you use a group of people to represent the elements of a system (people who know nothing about that system) suddenly this constellation seems to reflect the core issues of the relationships in that system, that organisation: the undercurrents suddenly become visible. Many books have been written about constellation methods, so we'll keep it short here. You can read more about organisational constellations in chapter II.6.

It is important to know that the constellations method has provided us with an enormous treasury of insights into how social systems function, what underlies their dysfunction and how this dysfunctional state can be transformed into one of health, flow and flourishing.

Clearly, organisational systems are different from family systems. This is why organisations deserve their own place: they are not just a particular kind of family system. Organisations keep society together, whether we like it or not, and all those organisations form a part of our societies, of our countries and of the world in which we live. Each of us is a unique part of our own family, but we all form part of our society and our world. Organisations sit somewhere in between, sometimes operating smoothly, sometimes stuck. Judgements and opinions form a part of us all. Organisations are subject to far more opinions and judgements than families. The phenomenological way of looking is one of having no judgement and wanting to change nothing. Of accepting the world just as it is. Strangely enough, facing and accepting reality, just as it is, often begins a process of change. Constellations have proven to be a good way to face what is.

This book is also about patterns. We are not always aware of the presence of patterns, or that we simply live in them and with them, as if we cannot do or know otherwise. Certain patterns, particularly unhealthy ones, can be persistent and stay in organisations for decades. Resisting patterns (usually in innocence of them) is a good way of ensuring they persist. What helps, is to face the truth and to take it as it is. Otto Scharmer, creator of the popular approach called Theory U, and a systemic thinker from the approach of 'learning' organisations, discovered that change starts with 'a shift in the inner place from which we operate'. By recognising patterns, facing them and taking them as they are (sigh… from my own experience I know this is easier said than done) such a shift in this inner place can take place. And then, sometimes, something totally new arises.

Sources for this book

This book arose out of encounters with hundreds of people, in more than twenty countries. People who run a company or work in or for one. People with a passion for their work that shows in new ideas, in satisfaction, in beaming with the feeling of being in the right place, in their strength and taking responsibility. A passion that sometimes translates into hate, incomprehension, tiredness, feeling stuck or feeling like a failure.

The encounters were with one-man or one-woman businesses, with small companies, with family companies – and all their complications – with companies that have grown since their birth to a couple of hundred workers and with globally-renowned multinational corporations.

Each of those companies is a kind of (little) miracle, with a beating heart – although the outside world might see it differently. I went to tanneries, banks, government organisations of every level, oil companies, supermarket chains, fashion houses, bicycle manufacturers, dentists, medical practices, universities and schools, sauna centres, consultants and helpers of every size and shape. So many different kinds of jobs exist in this world and how special they all are!

Many of these encounters with companies and their people were centred on a question they had about their organisation. *"How can we develop?"* *" How can I leave?"* *"How do I get justice?"* *"Which candidate should I choose?"* *"Is my son a suitable successor?"* *"Why are sales drying up?"* Each question imbued with a beauty and life force of its own, even if that life force expressed itself by wanting to give up.

The encounters and questions turned into hundreds of constellations, each one new, each one vulnerable. Often providing amazing insights for the issue-holder who brought the question, for the other participants and also for me. Insights that helped the company and the people to move forward, to become 'unstuck'. Such insights are an endless source of pleasure for me. Often I'd hear myself saying to myself, quietly *"Oh, that's the unique way only a systemic perspective can reveal what's really happening in a company"*.

These encounters took place in many different settings: constellations with a company's management team, often 'using' a small group from outside the company to represent the elements; open workshops or workshops with a specific theme such as Startups or Money and Investments. 'Guest' clients brought their questions into the hands-on modules of training courses such as Systemic Work in Organisations. Sometimes it was an individual coaching session, a telephone call, an email exchange or even a conversation on a plane. I experience systemic work and constellations as a very special way to meet a company or a country: I see attention and energy focused on a problem, discover systems that always have their own intrinsic movements and, always, there are people who really care about it and people who could not care less.

In amongst all the constellations, from thousands of students and participants in many countries, there were off-hand but sometimes profound questions (*"Oh, how I love those off-hand questions, that cut through everything, opening you to something much wider and deeper than before"*). I have found little that works so well as letting new insights emerge in a group focused on a specific question. This often lifts the whole field above the question.

I come from a family for whom companies actually 'do not really exist' or were seen as a 'necessary evil' or 'improper' or 'indelicate' (*"I notice that I am using the precise words that my grandparents and parents used"*). In a way I have become disloyal to my family as I have become more and more fond of companies. Because they fascinate me. Because it is a miracle how they work – and that they work at all. But mostly because they are worthy of my affection. We cannot avoid the simple fact that companies shape our society; in many cases even more than authorities and governments. This is a truth to which we all have contributed. Crises and prosperity both seem to result from the co-creation of large groups of people and big sections of society, in service to fields of enormous force.

Structure of this book

- **Part I.** General systemic principles for understanding organisations.
- **Part II.** Themes about organisational development, about changes and phases in the lifecycle of an organisation and an explanation of what constellations are.
- **Part III.** Seventeen chapters devoted to recurring organisational themes, such as contracts, fraud, investments, trauma, downsizing and mergers.

If you first want to read more about the constellations method, go to the second part of chapter six: Organisational constellations: methods, conditions and contemplations.

I hope you enjoy reading!

Jan Jacob Stam
Abries, France, January 2012

Part One

I

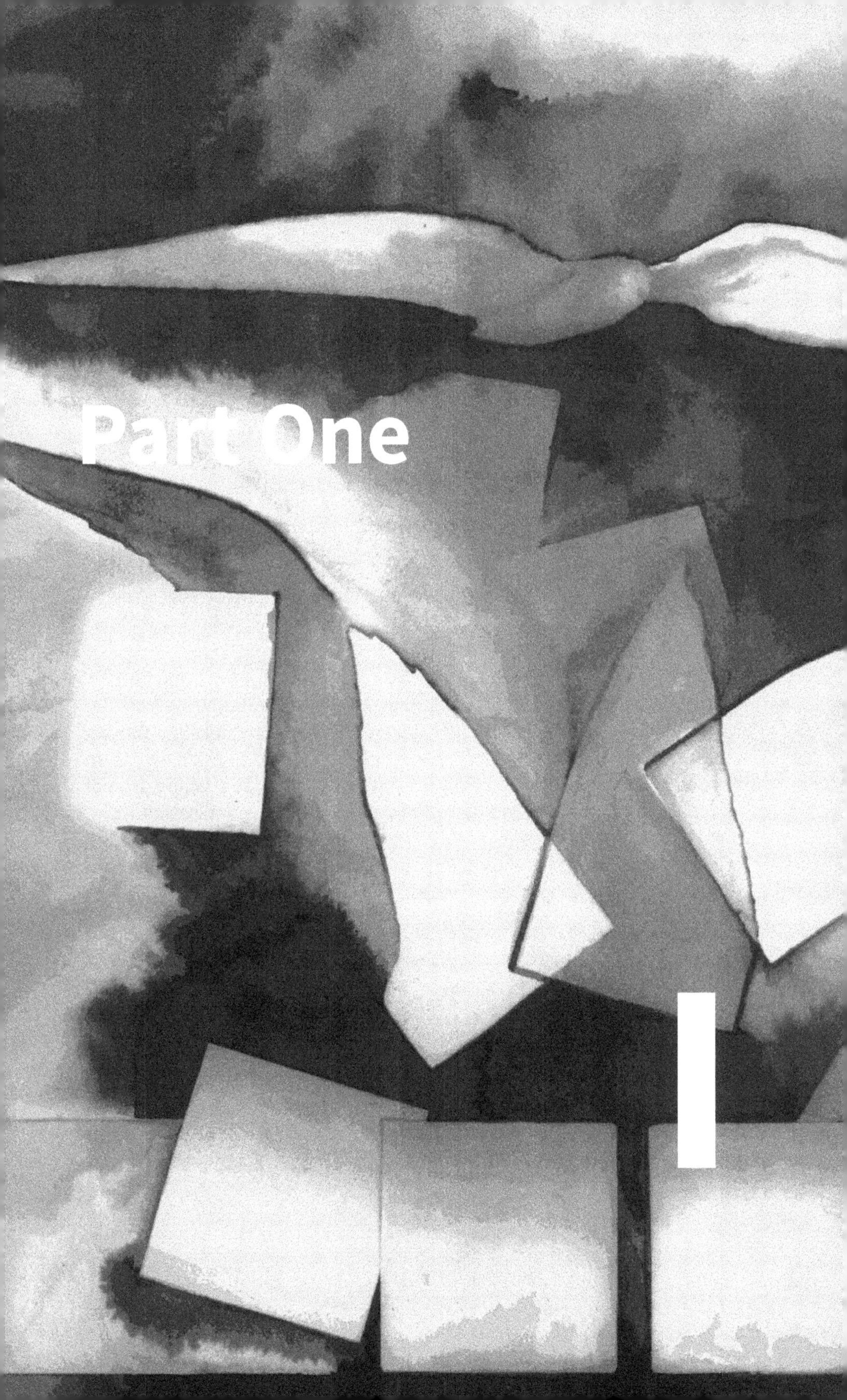

I.1 General systemic principles for understanding organisations

Fifteen years of systemic work, in organisations and other social systems, has brought to light a number of general principles that we see again and again. We've learned what these principles are, how they 'control' organisational systems and the conditions necessary for these systems to thrive.

Most practitioners work with three main principles, but in this book we introduce a fourth.

The four main principles:

1. Organisational systems want to be complete.

2. Organisational systems want to exchange with other systems, internally and externally.

3. Organisational systems look for and thrive with an intrinsic order.

4. The 'new' principle:
   Organisational systems want to reach their destiny.

Maybe it sounds strange, but I use the word 'want' deliberately. Not that we assume that an organisational system has an ego or a will, although that is perhaps true for those who are part of the system. But systems do have tendencies that prevail over the individual. Just as a falling drop of water or a soap bubble tend to move in specific ways, organisational systems tend towards specific, naturally-arising movements. These natural principles can, to a large extent, influence how an organisation comes into being, gets established and develops.

These tendencies or principles of how organisations behave have not been invented or constructed; neither are they the product of human will or fantasy. Through careful observation these principles were noticed and recognised as being intrinsic to organisational and other social systems.

I have often noticed that there is no need to explain to a director of a large organisation how constellations work or what systemic principles are. Sometimes they are surprised to see in images or to hear in words, what they had already unconsciously felt or understood about how those systemic principles work in their company.

There exists a kind of systemic intelligence, a sort of systemic wisdom that contributes enormously to whether organisations flourish or not during times of prosperity and hardship.

The fourth principle, organisations want to reach their destiny, I noticed and refined quite recently, during 2012.

Organisations have emerged from society and also want to achieve something in society and this desire is driven by larger forces than just a business plan or a leader's vision. It is about a kind of evolutionary force, with its own direction, that takes companies along with it. This development is far greater than the capacity of individual plants and species, even of complete ecosystems.

The destiny of organisations is about the larger developments in society: the force that brings about the death and renewal of communities, economies and social systems.

Hellinger calls this force spirit-mind, and many captains of industry know exactly what this is – although they might not call it by this name.

In the following chapters we will go deeply into the first three principles. Chapter II.5, examines, in detail, the fourth principle.

I.2 Systems want to be complete

Organisational systems want to be complete. This is a fundamental principle; not because this would be beautiful or good, but simply because it seems that it is their nature to want this. Every element that forms an organisation, now or in the past, has an equal right to a place in the system, forever. Even if this person, corporate culture, machine, department or production process is currently dysfunctional.

Similar to family systems, in which it does not matter whether someone is living or has died, for an organisation it also is unimportant whether an individual, a department, a function, a goal or a concept is still physically or temporally part of the organisation.

How is it then possible that an element, that once helped form an organisation, becomes excluded, is no longer a part of it? This happens when those in the system (organisation) want to forget it, or see it as a waste of time and energy, or talk about it in a condescending manner, or sweep it under the carpet. Whatever way is used to deny an element its rightful place, results in exclusion.

This need to be complete is often confused with the question of whether some aspect of the organisation is functional or dysfunctional. Naturally, the purpose of the organisation one hundred years ago is now likely to be out-dated and, therefore, dysfunctional. Society has evolved and now demands goals that are more relevant to these times. But this is very different to denying an 'old' goal its rightful place.

When exclusion works in reverse, so to speak, its effects can be even stronger. If an organisation hangs on to a goal that is now no longer useful, what is then excluded? The answer is… society!

Wanting to teach children something that was important thirty years ago, but no longer is, includes the old goal, but excludes the children's need for a modern, appropriate curriculum! Then, both the children's needs and the future are ignored, while teaching out-dated lessons en-sures that the school (organisation) stays in the past. This is an excellent recipe for inhibiting development or stopping it entirely.

Intermezzo: are you ahead?

Towards the end of 2010, as I returned from a six-month sabbatical, two eye-opening events happened to me.

The first was on a long plane journey during which I was watching a film called The Happy Housewife, based on a book by Heleen van Rooyen. Although I didn't know this particular book, I had read some of her other books and know her to be a very widely-read and popular author in the Netherlands.

Suddenly, in the middle of this film (about a woman with postnatal de-pression) my attention was drawn to a scene set in a clinic, where a group therapist suggests that the 'happy housewife' does a family con-stellation. The constellation is set up very realistically, with all the com-mon scepticism and awkwardness; during the constellation the wo-man's father suddenly appears. The rest of the film is about the woman's search for her father, who drowned himself when she was six, with his suicide being hushed-up by the mother.

I found it tremendously impressing, that a producer dared to use a family constellation as an important element in a film that would go on general release – with the goal of making as much money as possible.

The second event occurred during the doctoral ceremony of Wim Jurg, who has been researching 'branding' constellations for almost ten years. After Wim had defended his thesis, the most critical member of the doctoral committee remarked: "It's obvious that constellations work. That they are valid, reliable and offer a substantial and complementary method for brand research has been sufficiently demonstrated. Get started with it…".

What those two events told me was that if ever, perhaps unconsciously, I had intended to bring the constellations method into public awareness in the Netherlands then, thanks to many others, I had succeeded.

This realisation was accompanied by a little bit of shame. Actually, society had progressed further than I had (unconsciously) thought. I was still busy explaining to people what constellations are; that was necessary ten years ago. But not anymore! Time for new targets, new ambitions, new websites and, especially, a new attitude to society.

Are you ahead of society or is society ahead of you?

Goals

Goals are the pivot points between organisations and society. The goal is the lens through which society is viewed, but also through which society views the goal. When you have a goal, for example spreading your ideas by selling books, you are looking at society or at the emerging future of society, with the idea that society or a future society might consider these ideas to be a meaningful contribution. Society, also, is looking at you and your organisation through the lens of what you can contribute to them. Not only products and services, but also the forces and energy in these products. So, through the lens of the goal or mission, society and the organisation are constantly approaching each other, tasting each other, adapting and changing. Thus an organisation can grow, develop and adapt to society. In the Netherlands, housing associations were initially founded with the goal of providing low-cost social housing for people in need of a home. This goal was the driving social objective behind the creation of the majority of housing associations. Nowadays, however, this objective has almost vanished. Is it better, then, to end up with the phenomenon of housing associations in their current form, or to reorganise them in such a way that they can serve another purpose?

Organisations want to serve a purpose. If there is no purpose to serve then there is no movement that can reach its destiny; so the organisation loses its energy and dries up. It is often difficult for people to wind-up an organisation. Even so, it would be more powerful to bring to an end an organisation that has reached its destiny, instead of wanting to transform it into another kind of organisation. The force involved in ending an organisation liberates a significant amount of energy for something new. Often this is perceived as sociable unacceptable. But systems do not care much about what is sociable acceptable. It is, however, more damaging if we maintain something that no longer serves a purpose in society, as this is a recipe for excluding something useful or necessary.

By the way this also applies to maintaining functions, departments or sectors in an organisation, for example after a merger. If you keep a certain department or a function in your organisation that does not contribute to the whole, the people in this department or performing these functions will be and feel excluded. Their efforts and talents, instead of contributing, end in nothing.

It helps to understand that a goal can also bring about exclusion of someone or something. With a change of policy, for example, this can occur – yet go unnoticed.

Once, in an institution providing foster care, according to the person who described the problem, the organisation became neurotic after economy measures were initiated. Everyone thought it had to do with the cost reductions but, suddenly, the woman who had brought in the problem stood up and said: "*Oh! Along with the cuts there was also a policy change. Previously, we were allowed to support the foster parents and the biological parents. But, since the cost reductions, we are no longer allowed to work with the biological parents. They are now excluded and that has consequences for our organisation*".

How do you deal with the part of society that is excluded by the goal? By looking it straight in the eyes and accepting that the part you want to exclude is a part of the world as it is and has a right to be so. Looking into the eyes gives access to the soul, the essence. So an organisation working, for example, for the well-being and eventual release of political prisoners, could say something like this to their persecutors:

"Dictator, perhaps, by putting your adversaries in jail, you are trying to exclude them from your system, from your vision for your country. We, the organisation for the liberation of political prisoners, choose not to repeat this pattern by putting you in a mental prison. Your victims are just as much a part of your system as you are. We can see both sides. We know you are there and will always be there. Nevertheless, we will work for the victims of your system while looking you right in the eyes."

Actually their message could be: *"Please! Look! See that we do not consider ourselves to be bigger or better than you, therefore the forces in society are too big…"*.

In fact, something like this happened in Uruguay, after the era of dictatorship. The current president of Uruguay was a prisoner of the dictator's regime. His prison, for a couple of years, was a hole in the ground. After he was released and elected as president, he said: *"I do not feel like bringing the members of the dictatorial regime to trial. If we do that, it feels like revenge and we would be doing the same to them as they did to us"*. So the president chose not to repeat the pattern of the dictators, and most Uruguayans agreed, although the equilibrium was delicate. And still you can experience, walking the streets of Montevideo, how peaceful the atmosphere there is. Somehow they managed to grow beyond the tension of good/bad or perpetrator/victim. How different then, in some other countries, where society is still caught in the field of good and bad.

An organisation which chooses, as its goal, to fight against something, risks excluding a part of reality, if that against which they fight is not given a place in society.

I used to work in groups that fought for peace in the world. It was a shock to have to admit, in my fifties, following a work visit to Israel that war is a part of this world…

The more fanatically an organisation fights against something, the greater the chance that it will sustain and repeat the pattern that it resists. Inside many peace-organisations we can see expressions of violence. An

organisation that declares a war on terrorism, might create terrorist behaviour within the organisation and so imprison itself within the field of
good and bad.

It could be interesting, for a moment, to see if your organisation's goals
exclude some part of society.

And how would it be if you then face that part in your mind. Would
it make your organisation weaker or stronger? More grounded or less
grounded?

What does it mean when you say you want to be the best? While striving for this goal do you face and give a place to your competitors, the others in the field, or do you exclude them? How can a field, a market or an
industry grow in a more holistic way? When you face what is? Or when you
try to make your organisation the best – at the cost of the others?

Once, during a constellations session, a director of a Dutch bicycle factory wanted to see a picture of all the big Dutch bicycle manufacturers.
His intention was not to gain an advantage over his competitors, but to
see how the Dutch bicycle industry was doing in general and how it might
respond to the massive influx of cheap bicycles from China.

Competition is healthy and necessary. But when we choose to distinguish our company from our competitors by excluding them, we cause
problems for ourselves and for the whole field. The growth-supporting
form, for the field as a whole, is differentiation.

Differentiation means working from your particular strengths and doing or producing that which fits with your vision and, more importantly,
what you are good at. You still see, out of the corner of your eye, how
your competitors are different and how they are also in their strengths.
So, not only does the market become as large as possible, but also the development of the industry, as a whole, becomes optimal. When you want
to be the same as your competitors or when you want to put them out of
business, you take energy away from yourself and from your own business
rather than from your competitors. This makes the industry become 'more
of the same' and risks its collapse and the loss of its connection to society.

The desire of organisational systems to be complete applies not only to
the here and now, but also to the past. It especially applies to the founders,
ideas, groups of employees and products that, in the past, made the or-

ganisation possible and made it grow, survive and become what it is now. This idea also concerns elements that were not directly part of the organisation, such as clients who become bound to the organisation by purchasing its products.

Where, and in what way, are the original products and clients honoured or remembered? Are they mentioned in the company brochure distributed to new employees?

Failure too, belongs to the organisation. It has contributed fundamentally to its development. Without failure there would have been little risk involved. Facing failure means that a company was and is ready to push the borders, to cross them sometimes and to acknowledge that. This kind of risk-taking contains a lot of life force.

The organisation wants even the 'negative' events of its history to be included. The scandals, the frauds, the industrial accidents, the dangerous product defects; often swept under the carpet. They all form part of the history. The more the history is acknowledged as the only possible history, the less the chance that undesirable patterns will be repeated and developmental force will decline.

I.3 Systems want to exchange

Organisations are alive and, like all living systems, there are some things they cannot stop doing. One of them is exchanging: a continuous movement of giving and taking, or in fact: taking and giving. We will explain this later.

The engine of this exchange, which brings liveliness to a company and between a company and its market, is a permanent fluctuation, a dynamic imbalance between giving and taking.

At a micro level it works like this. Someone gives you something. You feel a pressure arise to give something in return. If you give a little bit more than you received in the first place, then the other feels a pressure to give something back, and so a steadily growing exchange in giving and taking begins. The root of the word pay is the same root as for the word peace. When you have paid, in whatever form, for something you got or took, the relationship is in balance again, in peace.

This is a systemic exchange among equals and a general model for lively, active relationships.

In organisations this exchange works the same way, although the turnover is not always represented by money. An organisation provides its employees with an income. But it also provides safety, the chance to be a part of something, to enjoy some status in a place where your talents can flow and are valued. In turn, workers offer their talents, their time, their involvement and reliability, creativity, sweat and passion. This exchange in giving and taking occurs just as much within the organisation as it does between the organisation and the outside world.

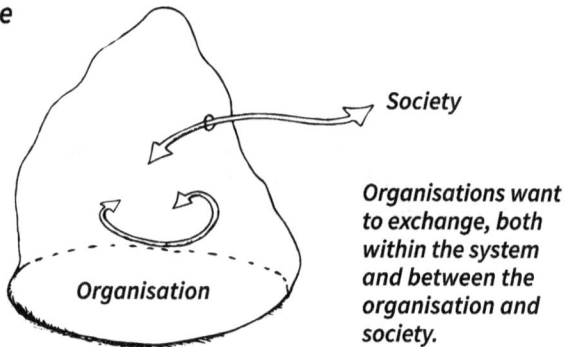

Exchange

Society

Organisation

Organisations want to exchange, both within the system and between the organisation and society.

Most commercial organisations supply products and/or services, and their customers pay for these. They do not pay only with money, but also by being constantly bound to the organisation, even if only for a short time as clients, from the moment that they make their purchase. For me, KLM does not only supply the possibility of transport: when I board a KLM plane, in a far away country, I feel a little bit 'at home'. For me this is an important reason to fly KLM.

People have a very precise sense of the balance of giving and taking. Just imagine what would change if, suddenly, your salary was doubled. Would you perform better, worse perhaps, or just the same? Would your performance be more rich and filled with your passion or more mediocre? Would you feel a greater or lesser bond with the organisation? Would it impact your dignity positively or negatively? Would you see your boss as bigger or smaller? Would there be more or less exchange; more or less flow?

Then consider these same questions if your salary was suddenly halved. Would you feel bigger or smaller? Would your boss seem bigger or smaller? And so on…

Interlude: secondary feelings

Let's take a look at guilt within the context of giving and taking.

First of all, there is a difference between guilt and feelings of guilt. Guilt is accepting what is: that one has given more and the other has received more. Full stop! That's it. It is a primary feeling, in contact with reality. It is a feeling between people, for example between colleagues and partners, or employees and managers. If guilt, the fact of an imbalance, can be faced and acknowledged, then the possibility exists to balance the debt. Sometimes this possibility does not exist. In this situation, simply acknowledging the debt as it is, without making any other claim, is a good way to move on.

If there are feelings of reproach about, for example, an unpaid bill or feelings of guilt about an excessive bill, then these are often secondary feelings. Secondary feelings tend to want to change the past which is, of course, not possible. Secondary feelings are linked with inner images and not with reality. It is possible to be occupied for the whole of your life with these kinds of feelings of guilt and reproach. Sometimes complete departments or organisations are under the spell of secondary feelings. One of the most common manifestations is complaining. Complaining about colleagues, about work, about 'the management who earn too much and are no good', about the government 'which doesn't lift a finger', and so on. Then there is no longer any systemic exchange and, consequently, very little life energy. It often makes for unpleasant relationships and feelings of isolation and lack of companionship .

Secondary feelings often have the following effect on people who want to help resolve situations like these. They really want to help, but the moment they reach out a helping hand they see and feel that they cannot help. Their helping movement will never reach the complaining per-

son; so the helper stops reaching out. So the movement of reaching out and withdrawing manifests in the helpers.

Helpers can often feel used, or see that the need for help, that they are addressing, is actually something else entirely.

If you want to help you can do so by realising that there are very good reasons for having secondary feelings. For example, because the underlying primary feelings are simply too painful to feel.

Example

For years I felt that I was treated unfairly by certain colleagues at a company where I worked for ten years as a consultant. When I left, I believed I was owed a considerable amount of money, but, through an accounting 'trick' it was not paid to me. Whenever I heard something about that company, I fell back into reproach and feelings of being treated unfairly. There appeared to be two underlying primary feelings. The first was the pain of relying on colleagues who are not there the moment you need them. The second, and that feeling was even deeper, became clear to me when someone asked me "Jan Jacob, how have you been able to maintain these feelings of reproach for 13 years?" *And I suddenly heard myself saying* "By loving that company so much…"

Escalation

In the previous paragraph we explained how the exchange in giving and taking can result in growing the turnover of a relationship or company. Also the relationship between two persons or an organisation and its customers will deepen and they will enjoy a greater bond with each other. But, in the movement of separation and hurt and taking something away from someone, there is also this exchange in giving and taking. If you cause someone trouble, or restrict him or her in their life in some way, or you take something away from them, then the other feels they have the right to cause you trouble in return. If what they do is more than what you first did (the first 'taking') then we have the beginning of an increasing imbalance, causing more and more trouble and pain. A clear pattern of escalation.

When such a situation occurs, the solution is to demand something from the other person – or to grant the other person something – but ensuring that what you 'return' is just not quite as much as what was given to you, taken from you or done to you. This restores the balance. To check if it really has been restored, just see if you can look each other straight in the eyes again. If you can do so, then both of you have become the same size again.

Bert Hellinger was, for many years, the director of a school in South Africa. One day a group of students did not show up for class, disturbing the atmosphere in the whole school. Bert Hellinger gathered these students together and told them they had harmed the school. He said "*You are allowed to come in again, but only after you have done something for the school to compensate for the harm you did. I'll wait for your proposal*". The students talked among each other for a while and proposed to clean the schoolyard. Bert Hellinger refused. "*That is not enough*". The students gathered again and then came up with the proposal "*We will paint the outside of some school buildings*". Bert Hellinger accepted, and the students started to work. When two-third of the buildings were painted, Hellinger told them "*Now it is enough, please come back in*".

When you forgive what the other person has done to you, this can make you feel bigger and the other feel smaller. The same is true when you say, after someone has hurt you, "*Forget about it*", or you cover up the incident. On the outside this move might look noble, while on the inside it gives you a position superior to the other person.

Exchange in family systems

Exchange in family systems is different from exchange among adults and in companies and organisations. Parents give and children take, and parents start by giving life. As children cannot give life back to their parents, they keep exchange in balance by giving life to their own children or by contributing to society or the community. So family systems are characterised by the one-way flow of giving and taking down through the generations.

Taking and giving in family systems

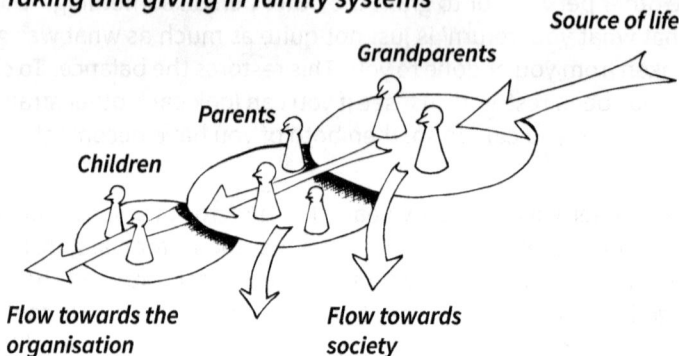

Source of life

Grandparents

Parents

Children

Flow towards the
organisation

Flow towards
society

It may happen that the family-system model of giving and taking appears, consciously or unconsciously, in an organisation. Obviously, this is more likely to happen in a family business than in a non-family business. An advantage of a family company is that employees feel a greater sense of belonging. If a company feels like a family then the unconscious message is that you must belong to a family system. Often we see that a family system (business) can survive loss or difficult times better than a non-family system.

But what happens if, for a long time, one gives too much to employees, making the imbalance in giving and taking too big? If they receive more than they can give, then they become smaller and feel a bit like children: sooner or later they will have to leave. A long-term imbalance among equals, in giving and taking, cannot be endured. The atmosphere becomes oppressive and exchange dries up. Inevitably, there will be a parting of the ways.

Not all collective agreements take this mechanism of exchange into account. Maintaining the balance of giving and taking is an art; not a particularly difficult art but one that needs more attention than just an annual pay rise.

Microcredit

What is the best size of a micro loan to provide maximum growth potential? When it is too much, the recipient is forever bound to the lender and becomes almost an employee or, worse, a slave. If the micro loan is too little to start even a very small business, it takes away the dignity of the entrepreneur and the energy for growth disappears.

Unemployment benefit and sick-pensions

What are the right amounts for unemployment benefit and sick-pensions? When does a payment help a person to bridge a difficult period and when does a payment oblige the person concerned to remain a victim or to stay ill? How can you prevent unemployment benefit being felt as receiving money from your 'parents' in a way that the recipient is forced into the pattern of a child? How much parenting by the state stimulates or erodes liveliness and participation in society? And when does it become a blanket under which the energy for growth withdraws? The same questions apply to grants, funding and subsidies. A newspaper recently published before and after articles about artists whose subsidies were abolished. Many of them displayed remarkable entrepreneurship in response to the changes in their financial situations.

Taking work with you

Sometimes it seems reasonable or appropriate for employees/partners to 'take' some of their clients with them, when they leave a company to start out on their own. For the company it is nice to know that there is some continuity for their customers. For the new entrepreneur it helps not to have a break in income and security. But one should realise that taking 'your' clients with you actually means you are continuing the old employer/employee relationship. The exchange in giving and taking between the former employee and the company continues for a while, and with it also come the patterns we described earlier.

Example

When I left a consulting firm, where I had worked devotedly for eight years, to start my own business, I suddenly learned that I had a competition clause in my contract. This meant that not only could I not do my new work with my 'own' clients and assignment givers, but also not for any clients from my old company. And the contract absolutely excluded taking existing assignments with me to my new business. That was a hard blow. Friends tried to cheer me up by saying that it would eventually work out with the competition clause, but a lawyer asked "Have you, as a co-owner, signed the contract in full knowledge?" "Yes", *I answered truthfully.* "Well", *said the lawyer,* "contracts are there to be respected and there is nothing I can do for you." *Looking back, that was the best thing that happened to me in the process of becoming independent.*

And that's what I call it, becoming independent. The road was, then, really clear for me to start from scratch and create something completely new. Potential clients? They started calling me. Actually long before I was ready. First I became a bit more independent; then entrepreneurship followed naturally.

Giving and taking

Although most people find it easier to speak about giving and taking, in that order, the exchange always starts with taking.

The first movement of a child is to take: the mother, the breast, the milk, life. It is an effort, a doing: then the giving can flow.

Starting with taking contains a risk: that maybe you cannot give back or give back enough. Just try… take something from someone while looking him in the eyes and when you are not sure you can give something back. Taking, in such a situation, is a bigger risk than starting with giving.

Entrepreneurship means facing this risk: that you might not be able to give back what you have borrowed. Accepting the risk gives strength. Strength that will be essential during the times of difficulty that will surely come.

Profit is not so difficult ato live with. When business is good many people like to participate and gather around the successful entrepreneur. But
facing the possibility of loss requires rather more strength. A kind of life
strength that later will benefit the organisation.

The following observation was difficult for me to accept… many companies, that are rooted in perpetrator energy, are often very successful
companies. Perhaps not so much because they have become rich in times
of war, for example, or at the expense of others, but because they know
(unconsciously) and continue to make the first movement of exchange.
The movement of taking.

I.4 Organisations want intrinsic order

> **"** *A horse does not know the notion 'I',
> only the notion 'we'. It does not have
> an ego. It does not matter for a horse
> where it is in the order of the herd, as
> long as there is order.* **"**

Introduction

This is going to be a relatively long chapter on order in organisations. Order provides the framework, the skeleton of the organisation. Order in
organisational systems is more complex than the other main principles:
completeness, exchange and reaching their destiny.

First we will look at the general principles of the concept of order. Then
we will go into more detail about the four main principles of order in organisations.

Some general principles of order

An organisational system flourishes only if, for each business unit, for each
department, for each function and for each worker, there is a clear and reliable place in the system. Clear means that there is no fuzziness about

these positions in the organisational system. The organisation provides a clear structure and holding space for, for example, a department. It is also necessary that the work of this department is useful and that the department is allowed to reach its destiny.

When this sort of order is in place, it gives a kind of peace and tranquillity. And because the order and tranquillity originate from a clear place in the whole, they make active exchange possible. The results are that people work in a healthy, pleasant and productive way, departments experience themselves as making a useful contribution to the whole and ongoing development flourishes.

So the more peacefulness that results from the systemic order, the livelier the exchange of giving and taking.

Once, in Brazil, I had an assignment from an important bank to do a day of constellations with the five directors of the strategy department. In less than a year there would be presidential elections. A consequence of these elections would be that all important directors would be either transferred or get new roles. The five directors knew that the hidden agenda in their team for this 'final' year, would be one of infighting for the best posts after the elections.

The Head of Strategy asked: *"How can we ensure, following the upcoming elections and the expected fights for the best posts, that we stay together as a team and continue to function well?"* If we put this into systemic language, it would be: *"The order of people is going to change. Most likely we will go into survival state for the next year. How can we ensure that enough clear order remains for the directors and departments to continue their work?"*.

I found it quite a courageous and conscientious question, on which we all worked with pleasure. A year later I heard that this constellation meeting was seen to have contributed very positively to the working atmosphere in the team during the restless year before the elections.

Order and hierarchy

Order is different from hierarchy. Hierarchy is more an organisational concept and mostly refers to the different layers in an organisation and usually, and implicitly, to the importance of the layers. Layers are either higher or lower than each other. This is most clearly represented in the organisation chart. Order, as we mean it here, is a systemic concept. It is about how different elements or subsystems of an organisation can exist next to one another and complement one another, in order to form the bigger system, the organisation as a whole. A whole with different properties than the sum of its parts.

So the systemic observation, that all systems are striving for an intrinsic order, has nothing to do with power, giving orders, the need for hierarchy or organisational charts. Order has to do with the need for a reliable place in your (sub)system, and for each subsystem in the whole. Order provides the anchor point in the outside world. There are many new forms of organisations arising, like networks, co-creating groups, self-organising teams. In each of these new forms, forms without hierarchy, bosses or power-struggles, one can still observe a striving for a kind of order.

The art of influence

It is an art to exert influence to the extent that appropriately reflects your position in the organisation. If someone tries to exert more influence than is appropriate to their position, they will be perceived as arrogant or authoritarian. Authoritarian people will have to work hard all the time to maintain their higher position. But meanwhile they often lose respect and, consequently, their authority.

Someone who holds back from influencing to their appropriate extent invites someone else to take the lead. If no one does, then the whole system weakens, runs the risk of collapse and the leader loses credibility.

Ordering principles

Up till now we have discerned four ordering forces in organisations. From least influential to most influential, they are:

- Seniority (page 26)
- Contribution to the organisation as a whole (page 27)
- Ordering by function (page 28)
- Ordering by guiding principles (page 38)

Seniority

Seniority has many different faces

1. *Age.* Age is probably the most important ordering criterion in families: respect for grey hair, the pater or mater familias. The oldest child, for example, is considered as first in line to take over a family business.

   When I was a 22-year-old teacher in an evening school for adults, I found it quite strange – in the beginning – that people much older than me were still prepared to learn something from me.

   How difficult is it sometimes for young professionals to be better than their older colleagues? Sometimes people feel too 'young' to carry a certain form of professionalism.

2. *Length of time in the profession.* When do you become senior? When my son was 26 he heard from his boss that he was now considered to be a senior consultant. But maybe this had to do with the fact that he wanted to resign and that his boss wanted to keep him. As a facilitator of constellations I still feel like a newcomer, although I've been doing this work, full time, for 13 years now. When I organise a congress or training, it is difficult for me to tell a colleague, with more years of experience than me, what I want him or her to do. *"Who do you think you are?"* is the little voice only I can hear.

3. *Length of time in the organisation.* People who have been there for long time know how everything works. They have also been through a lot; both good and bad. This might make their soul a bit less sensitive but it also gives a sense of their being rooted, and that demands respect.

4. *Length of time in the team.* For a new director, perhaps brought in from another company because of his proven qualities, it can be important for him or her to ask this question: *"Should I lead from the first position or from the last position?"* Guiding from the first position means taking the first place, from the first day, and stating which direction is to be taken; telling everyone what to do. There is no choice for the staff: the bottom-line is 'take it or leave it'.

   Guiding from the last position asks for an attitude of *"You, my team members, have been here longer than me. I would like to hear what you think works well, and is to be kept, and what is to be changed. Then I will make the necessary decisions".*

It should already be clear that this particular ordering criterion can easily cause conflict and division.

If, as a team leader, you would like to do a rather fine and simple acknowledging exercise with your team, you can ask them to sit clockwise: first in order of age, then in order of years of work experience, then in number of years in this profession, then in number of years in this organisation, and so on. If you really take some time for this and the employees feel safe enough to say how they experience these different orders, this is often felt as a very integrating process by the people in a team.

Seniority: things to consider

Women, returning to work after raising their children, often are offered a function that reflects only their work experience and qualifications before they took many years off to raise a family. How can the qualities they have developed during motherhood be acknowledged and be used beneficially by the organisation?

Is the organisation changed or improved by young people and their implicit knowledge about the emerging future, or does the organisation suck them into its existing patterns? How can the organisation benefit from the 'knowing' of the younger generations, without shaking-up the orders too much?

When elderly workers are valued, and have a good and enduring place in the system, a structure is created that supports young people, in the same organisation, to let their own talents fully flow. It makes a clear statement that it is respected and worthwhile to get 'old' in this organisation, instead of fearing being dumped at a certain age.

Contribution to the organisation as a whole.

An individual who 'saves' an organisation assumes a special place in the order. This can make it difficult to find a successor, because who can equal such a feat? Perhaps this is why a founder has such a special place in an organisation: they really have made a special contribution to the whole. And be aware, too, that there is often a 'founder' behind the founder: someone who, perhaps, invested money into the start-up company or who made it possible to create the organisation in some other way.

There are often many more people who contribute to the success of a project than you would think at first sight. Just take a significant achievement by your company and make a list of everybody who contributed to it. How many of them are clearly visible and recognised for their contribution and how many are in the shadows? And what is the effect if you take these people out of the shadows and put them in the spotlight for a moment?

There is a woman who takes care of the catering at our centre, but who also warmly welcomes the participants arriving in the morning after their long journeys. She finds the spotlight uncomfortable and tries to escape by saying *"It's just my job"*. But if you look closer you can see that she is beaming.

Acknowledgement of people's contributions has a huge bonding effect and makes organisations stronger, more connected and more resilient.

> **"** *How would it be for you and your organisation if your job description was 'contribute to the whole'?* **"**

Ordering by function

Here we come to an important principle of order. Let's take, as an example, a situation in a hospital. But, essentially, this could apply to any kind of organisation.

- In first place come the functions that create and maintain the holding space for the organisation as a whole, and make its existence possible. In a hospital this function is usually that of the economic director, who is in contact with health insurance providers and ensures that the hospital has enough money to operate.

- Then come the functions that are the core-processes of the organisation. In a hospital these would be the medical specialists.

- Then come the functions that provide the necessary information and tools for the core-processes: laboratories, X-ray departments and so on. A medical specialist cannot function well without the results of blood tests or MRI scans.

- And next come the functions that support the core-processes, such as the nursing staff.

- Finally come the ancillary functions that make sure that the core-processes and their supporting processes can function smoothly. The facility services, the cleaning, the housekeeping, the technicians, the administration, the porters, the food supplies and so on.

If we look at this as a scheme, as if it were a constellation, and we look at it from above, then the order looks like this:

Ordering by function; e.g. in a hospital

1 Director of strategy
2 Medical Specialist
3 Laboratory, X-ray, etc
4 Nursing staff
5 Facilities management, housekeeping, food etc

Clockwise from 1-5

Some remarks:

- Let's not forget that ordering by function is not the same as the hierarchy inside a company. From a hierarchical perspective, medical specialists will enjoy greater status than, for example, the cleaning staff. But from a systemic perspective, status has no place: each function is of equal value and equally necessary in the system as a whole.

- In the list above, those functions mentioned first have more agency characteristics and those mentioned later more communion character. (An explanation of agency and communion follows.)

- From a systemic perspective an organisation is a living system. The survival of the whole system has priority over carrying out the core-functions.

- Sometimes this appears to cause conflicts in an organisation, for example when either the medical director or the economic director has the leadership role. But both functions are equally needed. It is just that one function makes the framework for the other. If all goes well, they complete each other flawlessly and without tension.

Intermezzo: Agency and Communion

Agency and communion are like the brother and sister of each system. You could describe agency as the forces that guarantee the autonomy of a system and communion as the forces that make sure that there is bonding in a system. Ken Wilber is credited with naming these concepts.

Agency is like the Minister of Foreign Affairs. It takes care of the borders of the system, but without putting a fence around it. When someone not in the team enters a team meeting, agency forces ensure, depending on their strength, that the person either leaves the meeting or at least does not disturb it in any way. The people/functions in an organisation who are in service of the forces of agency are the ones in contact with the outside world. They keep an eye on their own territory, and on the whole playing field and they know precisely who might be possible collaboration partners.

Sometimes this can be felt in an organisation as the director being absent or unavailable. But, systemically, it is not possible for anyone to be absent. The question then is, 'Where, within the larger system, is the director?' In this case the answer would be 'In contact with the outer world, safeguarding and securing the borders of our company and its place in the market'.

Communion makes sure that everything goes smoothly in the system, that everyone feels comfortable and connected. It is analogous to the Ministry of Home Affairs. Communion makes sure that everybody feels acknowledged, feels seen and that there are rules in place that ensure cooperation within the system.

Each system needs these forces of agency and communion. The degree that either is important or needed can vary at different stages of the system's development. Take a moment to look at your own team. What are its relative proportions of the forces of agency and communion at this moment? How effective is the split? And what would, right now, make the team as a whole even stronger and more effective…more agency or more communion?

You can also ask these questions about the whole organisation. Recently I met with the director of a financial services organisation that was in a state of decline. Two roles were expected from her simultaneously. That she should ensure sufficient communion to guarantee their very high service levels and, at the same time, assume the agency role and find appropriate new partners with which to merge.

To help you imagine these ordering forces, some illustrations are presented in this chapter. The elements in the illustrations are viewed from above.

Agency

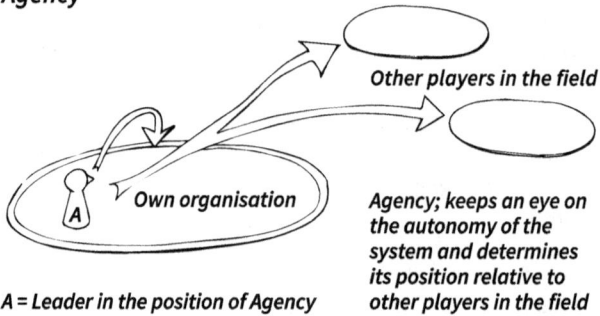

Other players in the field

Own organisation

Agency; keeps an eye on
the autonomy of the
system and determines
its position relative to
A = Leader in the position of Agency   other players in the field

Communion

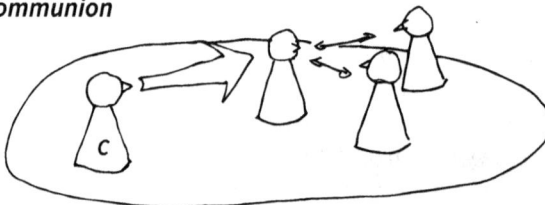

C = Leader in the Place of Communion position

Communion, takes care of bonding and well-being within the
department of organisation

What if there are no ordering forces at all or they are just not possible?

It seems that an organisation can continue without clear order for a while, but not for very long. A year or two seems the maximum. We have often seen what happens when people or departments, after searching for quite a long time, cannot find an anchor or reference point. For example after a reorganisation or merger. Then they start searching for another sort of reference point. This could be their professional skills and qualities. These are always with you, wherever you go, because your qualities and skills are inside of you. Then, when you feel that you have no firm ground or reliable place in the organisation where you are working, you can suddenly find yourself searching for work (still within the organisation) that you are good at or that you like. Then you no longer have a coherent organisation. In its place you have a conglomeration of individual entrepreneurs inside the company. Not that this is good or bad. But it is different from a coherent system

Some hospitals are deliberately organised in such a way. The medical specialists are actually entrepreneurs. They hire an office or consulting room in the hospital, book time in the operating theatre and hire the services of specialist staff and facilities. This kind of hospital is more like a health market than a consistent and connected organisation.

We saw something similar happen following a merger. The IT department no longer was sure of its place or legitimacy in the larger organisation. The IT team leader had approached his director for clarification and reassurance, but he could not get a decisive answer. So the team leader took it upon himself to go out into the 'new' organisation and promote the services of the IT department. When his department was not granted a reliable place in the organisation as a whole, the team-leader, himself, started to look for a good place for his department.

Not so long ago, entrepreneurship within organisations was in vogue. On the one hand this is a good concept: accepting the need to keep changing your role in the company again and again. In a sense to be regularly reinventing yourself to the organisation. On the other hand there is the risk that the departments are going to do what they are good at, find work that they like and where they feel appreciated.

As more and more departments become busy, independent islands, they can lose sight of what the system as a whole needs, bringing a loss of cohesion. This situation is neither good nor bad, but it is another way of organising yourself and it will have consequences for the organisation, its employees and its customers.

Intermezzo: Where is the client in the system?

Every organisation needs to consider this question. What is the place of the client in relationship to our organisation? Is the client where they are supposed to be or are they where we want them to be? There is often very little awareness of the possible positions for the client.

Here are some possible client positions. The diagram uses ordering by function to clarify, visually, the different positions of the client. Of course, the type of organisation is important. There are enormous differences between the customers of a supermarket chain, the patients of a hospital or the children of a primary school. The diagram below should allow you easily to check the place that clients have in your organisation.

Clients tend to feel better when they are seen by the organisation and when they can clearly see what the organisation offers. You can imagine the following positions of a client in an organisation:

Customer's position

Supermarket chain S   **Competitive supermarket
                                            chain X, Y and Z**

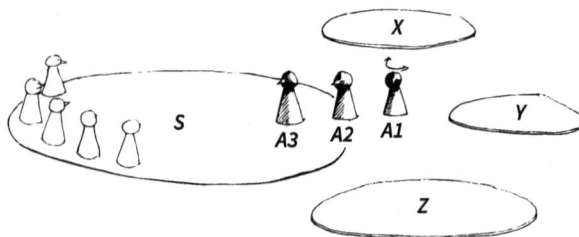

Position of customers relative to the services and products of provider S. A1, A2 and A3 show different possible systemic positions of customes (See text for explanation)

A. *An initial question is to ask yourself if the client is outside of the organisational system, on its edge, or a part of it.*

   A1) *The client is outside of the system.*
      The client feels free to choose who and what they want and can see other organisations offering similar products or services. The organisation sees this client as a doubter and makes efforts to reach or convince the client.

   A2) *The client is on the edge of the system.*
      Here the client already has a relationship with the company, feels a bond and loyalty, and will only choose for another company if he cannot find here what he is looking for.

   A3) *The client is in the system, is a part of it.*
      The organisation often finds this situation very agreeable: it feels good for the organisation that the clients are closely involved. But the organisation is not always aware that sometimes it can be oppressive for the client.

      The client's feelings of loyalty can change into feelings of being obliged, or restricted. In this place the client can also become a demanding client. Now that he has become part of the system, the client has the right to make demands and so becomes bigger than the organisation. The risk to the organisation is that it might lose its focus on potential clients who are still in the picture.

B. *The client is a functional part of the organisational system.*

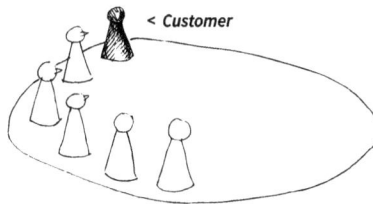

Customer is part of the organisational system

When, as a client, you are invited to help an organisation by think-

ing with its management, perhaps to make suggestions for improvement, but also enjoying a closer bond than just the buyer / seller process, then you become, temporarily, a part of the system. The organisation, so to speak, says to the client: "Join our club! Nice to see you again! We also have a customer card for you which gives your whole family a discount in our restaurant and it gives you privileged access to our annual sale. We are all one big family. Over there are some forms with a free pen; you're invited to make suggestions to improve our service and products. Have a coffee in the restaurant and use the free Wi-Fi. Don't forget to take a free lottery ticket; the draw is this afternoon, at five o'clock, next to the ball pit."

The client responds with "Well, that is a seductive offer, indeed! A nice day shopping, a safe place for the kids to play: how pleasant. But it would take rather a lot of time. If I want to buy something quickly I will go somewhere else."

C. *The client is in charge.*

Customer decides! "Customer is King"

My wife immediately said, upon seeing this position, "Oh! this is the Bonneterie (a famous Dutch fashion store). This is where the queen and my blind granny shopped. Once a year my granny went to the Bonneterie in order to be 'properly' dressed." *In this position, the client is king and also carries all the weight, power and status of a king. And this position also gives the client executive authority: he actually becomes a co-owner of the organisation.*

In a well-known consultancy firm it suddenly became clear that what they had always called being customer-focused, had changed, unnoticed, into a situation where the client was in charge. Seeing this led the partners to urgently reconsider their market strategy.

Of course there are endless variations of client positions. Rather than talk about it, it is much more fun to try it out physically. Place A4 sheets on the floor to represent the different parts of the organisation (as in the earlier schemes) and then try out the different positions of the client. You'll learn immediately how the client is feeling, how the organisation is feeling, how they see each other and how they would approach each other. It will give you immediate ideas about what your brochures and websites should look like. If you do it physically, by standing on the A4 sheets, you can immediately feel, in your body, the effect of the different positions.

Intermezzo: Shareholders

"What is the place of shareholders?" somebody asked Bert Hellinger in a seminar about entrepreneurship.

Bert answered "Well, the crucial question is whether the shareholders occupy the first or the last place? If they are last, then they support the company and willingly accept what the company does and achieves and they share in the profit. They do not interfere in policy, leaving it to the management. If the shareholders occupy the first place, then they 'take' ownership of the company. They are more focused on profit maximisation and the company is more focused on them than on society".

And then he added, softly "Maybe that's how the crisis in western society arose: because shareholders moved from the last place to the first".

Order in guiding principles

The order of guiding principles is the most determining order for an organisation. The guiding principle is the answer to the question *"what are we in essence?"*

I came upon it for the first time with the mayor of a town in Brazil. He wanted to know how he could best lead his management team of eighteen(!) directors. (In Brazil, the mayor of a town is also head of the civil service, but its directors are all nominated by the local political parties).

The mayor was accompanied by an advisor and by his wife, who was also one of the directors. Looking at the mayor, one immediately doubted his strength as a leader.

The symptom, in his organisation, was that each of the eighteen directors wanted to take the lead and that it was impossible to get them to agree.

While working, we did a constellation and everything suddenly became clear: there was a great deal of confusion about the order of guiding principles:

- Is our primary purpose to serve the citizens?

- Or is it to uphold the laws created by central government?

- Or are we a political arena for the next national elections?

Within moments of the mayor realising this he grew noticeably stronger: the advisor sneaked out of the room and the mayor's wife went to sit down in the last row. The mayor then said *"Thank you. Now it is clear. Now I know what I have to do"*. What he meant was: *"I first have to bring clarity in the sequence of guiding principles, instead of trying to bring order to my eighteen directors"*.

I remember this example so well because it makes clear how confusion about the order of guiding principles is often confused with lack of leadership. Lack of leadership occurs at a different layer of ordering, namely ordering by function, and not ordering by guiding principles.

A guiding principle is not exactly the same as a mission or vision. Missions and visions are constructs and need skilful and sustained communication to be spread, accepted and implemented throughout an organisation.

Guiding principles already exist. Sometimes they are outside of general awareness, but they are still present, embedded in the DNA of the organisation. All that is needed is to make them explicit and then to be clear about the actual hierarchy of guiding principles. The nice thing is, that as soon as the order of guiding principles is clear the need to communicate it evaporates. Everybody feels and understands it immediately.

In Jim Collins' book Good to Great he makes the observation that flourishing organisations are clear about their guiding principles. He goes on to state that he sees them as the most important criteria for success.

The idea of Guiding Principles works for all organisations, large or small. Individual professionals, with their own company or practice, can ask themselves what are their guiding principles. Clients and customers are especially sensitive to this. Also in a oversupplied market, clarity in guiding principles can make it possible to create your own profile and attract your own client group. Looking outwards it is an agency movement, looking inside it is a communion movement – bringing inner calm to the system.

Intermezzo: the guiding principles

I'm in Barcelona, delivering a training course, and I give the participants a quite difficult assignment: to identify the guiding principles of a number of specific companies.

Determining the guiding principles of an organisation needs a form of systemic observation. You expose yourself to the organisation and open up to the question "What guiding principles want to reveal themselves to me?" You also need to know the right questions to ask the company's employees.

At noon, I'm out for a lunchtime stroll and a fruit shop catches my attention. I decide I want to unravel its guiding principles. Everything looks so attractive in this shop. But what is it, beneath this lovely display, that makes the difference? I'm cautious, I don't want to hurry. The following day I come to this shop several times and I allow whatever wants to be visible to show itself to me. I resist making early conclusions and, suddenly, like a hammer blow, something becomes clear: there is nothing,

---

no barrier, between the products and the potential buyer. It is as if the fruits are connecting directly with the buyer. This isn't only because they are so attractively displayed. It is more a consequence of a guiding principle rather than that the display itself is a guiding principle. I go inside and say to the man behind the counter "It seems that there is nothing between your products and me, as a customer. What is the secret of your shop?" He laughs and says "It is true what you say and, besides, I have a good relationship with my customers". The truth of his statement is almost immediately demonstrated when a woman comes to the counter with several pieces of fruit in her hands. First she puts them on the counter and then she shakes hands with the owner. The order of the guiding principles became clear in this movement: first the woman chose the fruits she wanted (or the fruit let itself be chosen by her) without intervention or permission from the owner. And only then did she shake hands. "And also everything is really fresh" adds the owner, to me, speaking out the third guiding principle without being asked.

I talk with the owner for a few minutes and then he says "Do you like Indian food? May I invite you to have dinner at my home tonight with me and my Indian wife?".

How beautiful this is… I show my interest in guiding principles and a new friendship begins.

I have noticed that, most of the time, there are somewhere between two and four guiding principles that complete each other and dance around each other. Rarely more than four. If an organisation changes and the guiding principles change, then the question is *"are the new guiding principles compatible with the old ones?"*.

Some years after the privatisation of a Dutch telecom company, where I used to work, I heard the CEO say, in a room with a few hundred – mostly technical – employees, "*I don't care if, technically, the telephone system is old-fashioned … the clients want a dial tone*". He was actually announcing a complete U-turn in guiding principles, replacing technology with customer service. In that instant Dutch telecom changed from a technical company into a sales company. That his announcement came as a shock was evident by the shiver of disbelief felt by almost everyone in the room.

Hellinger adds a guiding principle via the question "*Is this company in service of life?".*

In service of life also means something like in contact with life and in contact with the community. When I first heard this statement I could feel, immediately, which Dutch banks were more in service of life and which were less so; which insurance companies; which energy providers and so on. It even led me to make some changes in the companies I use for these services.

Some more examples of guiding principles

A Steiner school in a village in Sweden was searching for the answer to these questions:
"Is our primary goal as an institution to:

- *Improve social cohesion in the village?*
- *Teach something to the pupils?*
- *Support the parents to educate their children?"*

In a regional college in the Netherlands their key question was: "First, is there a clear structure and, then, can we provide a good education? Or is providing a good education in first place with a clear structure actually being in service of a good education?" Confusion and lack of clarity around this, apparently simple, question appeared to cause tension and conflict in the organisation, on many levels and in many teams and to be a big energy drain.

How can one deal with lack of clarity in guiding principles?

(An example)

Over a period of two years, I had the chance to do constellations for several different managers and team leaders at the hospital in my home town. I noticed, in quite a number of those cases, that there was confusion about which took priority: the medical principle or the nursing principle.

I also am a client of this hospital, and stumbled again into this issue of guiding principles: my stepfather was coming to the end of his life and was ill and, despite the rigours of Alzheimer's Disease, he steadfastly insisted that he wanted to die at home, close to his beloved wife. Towards the end he had pulled out his urine catheter, damaging his bladder, and he was taken urgently to hospital. I went with him and stayed overnight; we were received well and surrounded with care. The nursing staff said to me "*This gentleman is going to die. If he wants to die at home, then he should go home now*". The treating doctors said to me "*This gentleman is going to die. First we will let his bladder heal until he is well enough to go home to die*". The nursing staff were desperate and so was I. As a member of the patient's family, I had a much clearer bond with the nursing principle than with the medical principle.

In this same hospital a head nurse came to me with the issue of unity in her team. Tension had risen after introducing nurse practitioners: nurses who are allowed to carry out very specific medical interventions. No longer 'just' nurses but also not doctors. Despite the good intentions of all the nurses it was very difficult to maintain a good atmosphere and collaboration within the team, as the team also included 'ordinary' nurses working beside the nurse practitioners.

Finally, the head nurse could see the issue clearly: the tension – in the team – had nothing to do with the people who worked in it. It was caused by the ambiguity and division – in the hospital – about the order of guiding principles. "*Are we, in the first place, in service of the medical principle or of the nursing principle?*" Or more directly "*Are we in service of length of life or quality of life?*"

The issue needed to be addressed by the board of directors. That was its correct place. And, of course, the head nurse was not in a position to solve the issue of hierarchy of guiding principles. She could also see that applying more force and authority within her team would not help resolve the situation.

Her next, and very logical, question was "*What now?*"

Conflicting guiding principles

What remains unresolved at the strategic level is repeated at the executive level

Here is a possible solution, one that begins as an inner process. The head nurse inwardly assumes her agency role, goes to the board of directors and says *"Apparently this hospital is divided about its guiding principles. In my position I cannot solve that. So I will stop fighting against this vagueness and also against you".*

First movement by middlemanagement

Senior nurse A acknowleges the lack of clarity in guiding principles

Then she goes to her team and says *"There is vagueness in this hospi-*

tal about guiding principles. We all feel it and we notice the effect it has on our team. I cannot solve this for the organisation. I know it is there and I acknowledge its existence and also how, at times, it divides you, even if you do not want it to. What I can do and will do is to ensure that it ceases to be your problem, and I will do everything in my power to create the best environment for good cooperation within our team".

Second movement by middlemanagement

Senior nurse A creates the holding space for collaboration within her department

Systemically this intervention means:

- That the head nurse does not put herself above the board of directors, allowing her team to take its natural place in the order. It is not their task to resolve strategy issues.

- That this, previously unrecognised, lack of clarity about the order of guiding principles has been brought into general awareness. Unconscious confusion, especially, makes teams restless and disconnected. The moment everybody becomes aware of a pattern, the more easily it can be handled.

- That the team leader, by assuming the agency role, can create a framework and holding space that enables the team to work well, without losing contact with higher management and the rest of the organisation. Her action avoids divisions occurring. Sometimes you can see the following happen in teams. In order to continue functioning when there are unresolved issues at the strategy level, a team says *"We must separate and make our own sub-system; let's put a fence around our department"*. Systemically, this is understandable, but creates an organisation where the sum of the departments does not lead to a greater whole. Clients, and in this case patients and their families, are the ones who suffer in this situation; they feel pushed from pillar to post.

- By acknowledging at which level of the organisation the issue belongs, without feeling superior to that level and its members, repetition of the pattern in the team is prevented.

Middle management

One of the systemic tasks of middle management is to handle lack of clarity in guiding principles. This is an important and possibly underestimated task for middle management. It demands that you mobilise your agency forces to ensure your department has a proper place in the organisation, while applying your communion forces to give it a good working atmosphere. And you must do this in a field where you are constantly under pressure, from everywhere in the organisation, to deliver. The board want you to implement their new change process; the employees want clarity about their roles and responsibilities; other departments need workflows to be maintained; dissatisfied clients want resolutions and on and on and on it goes. Actually middle managers are asked not only to be 'artists' in their fields, but also 'artists' of the Field.

I.5 Systems want to reach their destiny

That systems want to reach their destiny arises more frequently in organisations, however large or small, than in family systems. Destiny is something more than a goal or an objective. Ultimately you could call it the fate of the organisation. When we say that organisations want to reach their destiny, we mean that organisations want to move and affect something in society. Under the umbrella of destiny people can have several goals, for themselves and/or for the organisation.

People die when they come to the end of their lives no matter what form that end takes. An organisation, however, ends when it reaches its destiny. An organisation changes something in, and adds something to, society and at a certain moment that work is done. Of course, how long that takes depends on the kind of organisation and the nature of society at that time.

The fact that organisations want to bring about or change something in society means they have a particular direction, and that they create something means they have a creative force. Destiny can be seen as an intrinsic movement in an organisation with a creative force. Organisations are constantly making something new. Perhaps not only because that is the best market strategy, but also because the phenomenon of organisations has arisen to help shape society. Organisations are, as it were, taken into service by a larger creative evolutionary force.

This means you can view an organisation as a bundling of creating forces that share the need to reach a destiny. Imagine how you would feel if the work you do, the creative force that flows through you, had no effect anywhere in this world, changed nothing, resulted in nothing. Your work would quickly become a very dull affair. The idea that work can reach its destiny can perhaps be illustrated by the phrase to add meaning to, and this is clearly on a totally different level than achieving goals.

The reaching for destiny of a person's or organisation's work is a different movement than the exchange of giving and taking. Giving and taking is important for a system as it ensures interaction and turnover, but that is of another order than the fulfilment of the organisation's destiny. Actually, destiny and the creating force in an organisation are one-way traffic (as opposed to the balance of giving and taking). In this context, destiny is about changing something in society without immediately seeing or receiving anything in return.

I remember well how it felt when I suddenly realised, after some years of teaching, that I would never know how most of my pupils would live their lives. I would never know if my work as a teacher reached its destiny. Immediately after I realised this, I felt just fine: it was okay not to know this. And it is precisely this inner acceptance that allows the movements in peoples' work and in organisations to reach their destinies. A willingness not to measure one's effect on the whole. Being in contact with the destiny of your work but not claiming it as yours. It is this that makes modest companies great; just doing what they have to do. Not out of ego, but because society seems to have taken you into service for this. When a person or a company is in contact with their destiny, they beam and radiate with a special glow.

If you took this idea seriously, you would see organisations as social movements. How would this change our perception of organisations?

And, thinking of destiny and its evolutionary force, how would we look at society as a whole? Society taken into a movement by larger forces then society itself? Forces that can both create and destroy?

At this point I would like to describe a spontaneous constellation process that arose at MIT (Massachusetts Institute of Technology), Boston, in October 2011.

For two days, eleven people came together to explore the possible synergy of two different systemic approaches: Theory U and Systemic Phenomenological Constellations Work. Our only prior agreement was that this would be two days of experimenting. The eleven were all pioneers in one or other of the approaches; people who had been involved for a long time. Everyone understood the need to be really there: to be completely present and to be open to whatever might arise.

We're in the second day and Otto Scharmer says he would like to explore if a constellation can show the form a possible new phase in society might take. He talks then about his idea of a society that could arise as an answer to the emerging future. He calls it Society 4.0. In Otto's model, Society 1.0 is a centralistic society; 2.0 is also centralistic, but with the added factor of a compartmentalised or divided society and 3.0 is a network society. That is more or less where we are now. But it is, as yet, unclear what Society 4.0, the future society, will look like. Otto allows himself to be guided by the three big divisive forces that he sees at the moment in society: he calls them the ecological divide, the prosperity divide and the spiritual divide.

Spontaneously, within our group of eleven, we begin to represent elements. One person says she will represent those people living below the poverty line (we'll call them the poor). Another then steps in to represent the mothers of the poor. Then someone for the earth, and somebody for all the people who commit suicide (at this moment twice as many people kill themselves than kill others, including in wars). Soon, other elements assume a place: religious institutions; education; governments; multinational corporations and banks. China arises, apparently as an increasingly important factor. Then the 'final' element appears: the emerging future. The constellation starts to move and develop. The suicides creep into a corner. The poor find another corner. The religious institutions stand, for a long time, as if paralysed. Government stands on a chair, and the multinationals respond by standing even higher, on a table, and the banks are interested only in the actions of those two. Throughout the constellation, education tries to make contact with many elements, but none of them really listen to it and it cannot find a stable place. China is very present but hardly moves.

As I represented the multinationals, it is easiest to describe the whole process from 'my' perspective. In the beginning I looked down on government, and also down on the banks, but without revealing my view of the banks. I noticed two constant feelings or factors, during the whole constellation. One was my sincere conviction that I was doing something good for society. The other was how my attention was drawn to places where there was liveliness, life force. That's where my chances were. My most important value was my autonomy, because with that I would be free to move where I wished. My fear was of not being needed anymore, becoming redundant or being left-out and no longer able to participate in the whole thing.

And then a new development occurred in the whole constellation: the emerging future, which had stood to the side for most of the time, began doing something strange. For a long time it was unclear what, but it seemed to involve water. Then it started distributing small cups of water. And this simple act caused something significant to be felt by the other elements; it was almost unnoticeable, yet unmistakable. Later, when the constellation had ended itself, the governments, the banks, the multinationals and most of the other elements said: "*Suddenly we realised that our role in society would change. We felt that we wanted this and also that we agreed with it, even when it felt more like 'being taken by the hand' than a conscious choice. It became clear that for us, it was about giving meaning to society. But how, precisely? For a moment it seemed as if that would have to crystallise. But suddenly it seemed possible that the different ele-*

ments might really begin to see each other in a 'new' way, without opinions or prejudice, and create a completely different cooperation and society". We stopped there. Afterwards each element recounted his or her journey during the constellation. That took three quarters of an hour. Forty-five minutes with everyone's full attention and presence. Their stories were far too full and impressing for me to take it all in or to document here. But we all shared the awesome feeling of having seen, felt and experienced a glimpse of a new, and radically different, society.

So, who knows what has the ability and desire to reach its destiny.

> " *Life wants to produce life and that seems also to be true for organisations: organisations want to produce life.* "

Jan Jacob Stam

Part Two

Organisations constantly want to move on, to develop, to conform to society or to be a step ahead of society. How to take a systemic look at this process of moving and developing is the subject of Part II.

It follows the developmental paths of an organisation and examines that development from a few different angles. Some of these perspectives might help us to see the organisations, in or with which we work, in new and different ways.

II.1 The lifecycle of an organisation

Each organisation starts with an idea

Sometimes an idea of your own and, sometimes, mostly unconsciously, an unfulfilled idea from someone from your personal history. If, for whatever reason, this 'someone' was unable to fulfil his or her dreams and ambitions, their drive can start to flow through someone in a subsequent generation. The original person, who could not fulfil his or her own ambition, becomes the founder behind the founder. Many times I saw that when a person chose for their first vocational study after school, it was precisely that which someone else in their family system could not do or could not finish or live fully.

Sometimes the germ of an organisation can be formed, also often unconsciously, by promises we make to ourselves as a result of events we witness or experience in our own lives. Once, a Brazilian woman was visiting a slum, accompanied by a guide. She saw that the young children had bitten-off nails. "*So young, and already so many worries*" she said to her guide. "*No! Rats bite off the nails of the children during the night*" responded the guide. At that moment the woman made an inner promise concerning her professional life 'no child will be in such a position again'.

As you see, these sentence often come up in you as if an other voice is speaking, as if they come more through you than from you. Often these sentences have no limitations. When part of the sentence is 'No child...' this can mean 'no child in my country', or 'no child in the world'. These are pretty big promises, often hard to fulfil. Years later, this lady became the president of the Brazilian state bank and one of the cornerstones of her leadership policies was that the bank must offer a lifeline to poor people.

In another example a child sees other children being bullied in the schoolyard. Immediately, she promises to stop this ever happening to any child again: following her studies, she becomes a teacher.

One day, as a young man, I found myself riding along a bike path looking down at a fascinating pattern which had developed on the surface. I still can remember the inner sentence that came up that moment "*someday I will unravel the riddle of patterns*". The seed of a desire to understand the secrets behind patterns in living systems was sown. That this seed led me to study biology seemed logical to me, but I could never have guessed that it would take me on to constellations and systemic work.

Such an idea, the seed of an organisation, is an answer to a need or message from society; an organisation can only grow and succeed if it is always in contact with society.

Sometimes, though, we are simply taken into the service of something bigger, something greater than us or our individual hopes and plans.

Goals

The goal is the fulcrum of the relationship between an organisation and society; it gives force and direction and has its own focus. It wants to achieve some things but not other things. Look for how much yes is there in the goal and how much no: too much yes makes the organisation lose it's strength and too much no frightens clients away or makes the organisation appear exclusive, above society. When we make a decision, we say yes to something. But in that decision we also say no to many other possibilities. Often it is easy to say yes, but much harder facing the consequences of all the noes. The strength in a decision comes from the hard part: facing the noes. Sometimes it is the other way round: saying no is easy and saying yes is painful. For many people it is much more painful to say yes to your own greatness and potential, than to remain small. So we see that the balance between yes and no is important.

The guiding principles provide the answer to the question "*What are we in essence?*" and they help to balance the yes and no energies.

Then the organisation has to find its shape. The original idea becomes concrete: a product or a service. To whom or what will the clients react?

To the product/service? To the name? To the person who is selling the product or delivering the service? Are the guiding principles obvious to potential customers and are they attracted by them?

Now all the functions needed by a start-up organisation must be fulfilled. This does not mean that you have to define them all, create a tasklist and find a person for each function. In the beginning, almost all tasks are shared between just one or two people.

Only and precisely the most necessary functions, and it is an art to sense exactly what is needed. How much agency is needed and how much communion? How much time and energy do you spend on the agency-functions such as marketing, on the communion-functions, and on the core functions of the organisation? And, finally, in which functions do you need to invest skills, energy time and money?

Sooner or later, that exciting moment arrives when the system changes from one person, or a group of passionate people, into an organisation: from a system of people into a system of functions. I remember well, some years ago, answering the phone in our office and, without thinking, saying *"Jan Jacob Stam speaking"*. There was silence at the other end of the line and I thought I sensed disappointment: *"Oh, I thought I called the Bert Hellinger Institute..."* was the hesitant reply. I felt irritated as these words arose within me but weren't spoken, *"I thought I was the Bert Hellinger Institute"*. Later that evening I finally got the message: *"Ah, this means we are no longer a group of people and have become an organisation!"*.

Growth

What does growth mean when we look at it systemically?

Growth can mean that the organisation becomes increasingly more rooted in the community. What the organisation delivers adds meaning to that community and, in return, the organisation takes its meaning from that community: so both are growing. The better an organisation is rooted in society, the more resilience it develops to cope in times of crisis.

Growth can mean a more-intense exchange in taking and giving. More intense need not mean a higher turn-over in numbers, but an increased quality in the exchange, often resulting in a stronger bond between the organisation and the market.

Growth can mean a stronger position in the hierarchy of companies in the neighbourhood, in companies doing similar business, and of concepts that were there already earlier in society.

In the early days for example, in many countries, there was a backlash against family constellations (the therapeutic branch of systemic work) attacking it on the basis that it had jumped to the front of the queue, ahead of existing approaches such as constructivist system therapy.

On the surface we saw this backlash expressed as substantial clashes between practitioners of either approach but, when we looked deeper, we saw a disturbance in the order. It seems that introducing a new concept, even if it fits current society perfectly, has a greater chance of being accepted and respected if it takes its appropriate place in the order of concepts.

Growth can mean more of the same: constantly improving in what you do, while constantly growing along with society. Companies evolving this way grow in reputation and reliability and can function well for a very long time. Take a look at some of the companies around you or in your country and see which fit this description.

Growth can mean diversification. Let's look at the example of a major drinks manufacturer and its alcopop product. For over a hundred years the manufacturer had been distilling an excellent gin, but wanted to enlarge its product range by introducing alcopop drinks.

Systemically seen, diversification needs the permission from all the past and current customers who bought and drank the gin: we could call them the systemic shareholders. Often there are many more shareholders than the obvious ones. Former owners who left the company, somehow can still be in the DNA of the company, and it needs their 'permission' or 'blessing' to make a big change in the company. The same applies to former customers who, through buying its products, helped the company to grow.

An important question here is whether the guiding principles of the new product line, the type of product and the kind of energy it has, fit with the existing product line. If that is not the case then, systemically speaking, a new company is being created. If this is what is desired then it is worthwhile exploring whether it would be best to put both companies into one holding company, or to register them under the same name, or would they be better under different names and so on.

Finally, growth can also take the form of downsizing. Then the essence of the company gets priority over profit, employees and products. Growth meaning here: more focussing on the essence of the company. Peeling away everything that does not belong to the core of the company.

A company's end-of-life

What determines when a company has come to the end of its life? Mostly it is when the company reaches its destiny; has finished its work in society. Sometimes it is when an entrepreneur, running their own enterprise, has reached his or her destiny and knows or feels that this particular work is complete.

By the way, destiny and finishing are completely different to retiring and handing the company over to a successor. When an entrepreneur has finished with an enterprise, (even if he or she is not yet aware of this fact) the employees can feel that the entrepreneur's attention is somewhere else, that he or she has been taken into the service of something new.

II.2 Change from a systemic perspective

Some thoughts about change

The beginning

Change begins with an idea. It would be useful to check the source or worldview from which this idea (for change) originates.

Does the idea originate in the feeling that "*the world is not right*", or does it have it's roots in i"*the world is fine just as it is*"?

Does the desire for change originate more from the will, from what the system requires, or does it resonate more with the destiny of the organisation?

Change in resonance with the will

If I want to change something, I can make a plan and I can carry it out. The force for change does not only come from the plan itself, but also from me. To see a plan through demands dedication and strength from me from the moment the plan is implemented until it is completed.

An example

We have a publishing business which was in decline for a while. Largely this was because my personal input and enthusiasm had also declined. In the beginning I really enjoyed learning how to start up a publishing company. We visited the Centraal Boekhuis in Culemborg (the main logistics provider to the Dutch book industry) to learn how book distribution systems work. We talked with bookshops about their purchasing policies and we investigated the value of exhibiting at book fairs. With a lot of pleasure and energy, and surprisingly smoothly, we launched our publishing company. When it went into a bit of a slump I realised that my personal contribution, my enthusiasm for the project, had diminished. I'm pleased to say that new life has been breathed into the business by an enthusiastic secretary with commercial acumen and some passionate translators. Their will and strength and energy continue to push the company forward again.

Change in resonance with the system

The system can be inside the organisation or it can be the greater system of which the organisation is a part. When the system around our organisation changes, for example because of new regulations, or because societal needs change, then we have to change how our work relates to the greater system in order to continue delivering whatever it is for which we, as an organisation, were taken into service. You could say that the organisation, as a whole, is in service of society. When society changes, then what we provide should also change and this, in return, will change our internal system: functions will change, products will change, projects will end and new ones begin.

Book selling was, and is, declining anyway: e-books are the growth market and the profit margin on books is getting smaller every day. We can't ignore this, so we adapted and created an online store. Supplying e-book versions is the next logical step and that is in development. Initially, the goal of our publishing company was to translate selected books, about constellations and systemic work, from German to Dutch.

After a while, experienced Dutch facilitators began writing and so we edited and published some of their books.

If the purpose of the publishing company was to bring systemic work in the Netherlands into public awareness, then that goal was reached in 2010. That could have been reason enough to have ended the publishing business there and then, and that was considered…

Change in resonance with destiny

What is the destiny of society at this moment? European society, Western European society, Dutch society, our town and village societies?

What is the destiny of our organisation? Has it been achieved? Is there still something left to do, and for how long? When we no longer resonate with 'our' destiny, then symptoms such as loss, inefficiency, illness or staff turnover begin to appear in the organisation. From the 'spirit-mind', this evolutionary force which is in service of the development of society as a whole, we try not to resolve the symptoms, but use them as pointers to where we have deviated from our destiny, and then take swift and appropriate action.

… but it felt like the publishing company had not yet reached its destiny. Although a considerable number of books had been sold, it felt as if there was still a lot of life force that wanted to flow. Business is now on the upturn, reflecting the way the whole field of systemic work is deepening and broadening. Systemic work from the spirit-mind is a deepening with considerable consequences. Social questions are arising, eagerly inviting us to look at them from a systemic perspective. Authors

JAN-JACOB STAM

*are using this perspective to address these new social issues. We see
the tone and direction of the books changing. In the beginning, they offered the reader a chance to learn from experienced practitioners and
experts. Now, the focus is on the broader pallet of sharing experience
and knowledge, and is heading in the direction of books that invite us
to some form of co-creation. So, for us as a publishing company, it looks
like 'our' destiny has unfinished business with us, that it continues to call
us into action.*

When the desire to change something comes from an urge to recon-
struct the world, it requires a great deal of effort and maintenance (a main
law of thermodynamics). Change in resonance with destiny, even if you do
not know what destiny, requires awe and admiration as its energy source.

What do you want to change?

Changing structures and processes requires directorship.

Changing guiding principles requires leadership.

Changing a 'field' requires wisdom.

When to initiate change?

The ancient Greeks had two words for time: chronos, for the idea of time
as a planning and measuring device, and kairos, for the idea of the 'right'
or most-opportune moment. Which one do you use for your change planning? Chronos we know well. We use it for project planning and critical
path analysis, and it is there every day in our agendas. Chronos works
well with our strategic plans and our financial milestones. But kairos and
chronos don't always get on that well together. Kairos has a habit of pop-
ping-in unexpectedly. Not only is it a bit less reliable than chronos, it
doesn't hang around too long either. Each kairos moment comes by only
once. Notice it and act without hesitation. Kairos doesn't bang on your
door: you feel its presence. To catch it you need to be close to your intuition, some distance from the issue – and it helps to be a little out of focus.

Can you change a Field?

Morphic fields, as named and described by the eminent biochemist, Rupert Sheldrake, tend to repeat their patterns, in the same way as fractals. Some fields are strong and resist change vigorously: the Netherlands' fields of education and medicine are examples of strong morphic fields – even though the latter has become more open over the last few years.

Changing a field requires an impulse from outside. Even a crisis will do, as long as it is strong enough. So if you want to change a field, or a field is needing a change, where from outside does the impulse originate? Are you open to these 'wake-up calls'?

But it is also possible to make the field fluid from within itself, to enable it to re-organise itself. Theory U people do that by coming together as a group and then consciously letting go of their patterns, and by giving their full attention and sensitivity to the here and now. This is called 'presencing'. Within such a fluid field there is a source; we can call it essence. Once a field is fluid, from this essence new thinking can develop, new ideas or patterns. It is important to stay in contact with that source, as the new ideas begin to crystallise by trying out and implementing the new ideas, concepts and thinking.

In the earlier description of a social constellation example at MIT (chapter I.5), the combined group of systemic workers and researchers from the Presencing Institute came up with a new guiding principle for emerging society: 'To add meaning to society'. Although, at that moment, nobody in the room could say what this actually meant, or put it into concrete terms, they all could feel its presence as a source around which new patterns and possibilities could coalesce in the future.

What might you encounter on the path of change?

Resistance

Resistance is, actually, being loyal to something precious, something valued in some way. When this is not acknowledged, people identify with what they cherish and fear will be lost in the change process. The more the valued concept or machine or business process is threatened by change, the stronger their identification becomes. When you can see resistance as loyalty to something precious, then you can also begin to see what it is that really is precious. Then you can separate this from the person or people who are protecting it. This makes the change process more manageable for everyone.

As an employee you can also identify with this. If you feel resistance to a proposed change, ask yourself: *"What is my resistance trying to tell me? What principle, important to me or the organisation, is threatened in some way?"*. It also helps to remember that although you have the principle, you are not the principle.

Patterns

Patterns tend to repeat, and the more you want to get rid of them the stronger they become. It seems that patterns do not like being dumped, ignored or excluded. When we try to do so, they return, sometimes sneaking in again, unnoticed, through the back door. What seems to work is consciously letting go of patterns: for example by facing the pattern, holding it in your awareness and considering, for a moment, when and how this pattern served you well. Perhaps it supported you or your team to act quickly in a certain situation. When patterns are recognised this way they tend to withdraw: they don't actually go away, you just don't need them anymore.

The art of letting go requires accepting that moment when you find yourself suspended in a vacuum. You've released the old pattern but a new one hasn't formed yet. In critical situations you will tend to revert to the old pattern, or rather the old pattern will jump in to fill a familiar gap. Releasing a pattern means a moment of total loneliness, standing in the unknown. And in that moment you cannot be sure that a new pattern or orientation will come. You are taking a big risk in letting go. However long or short your visit to 'limbo', it helps to endure it and, if possible, to see this lonely place as a friend.

Unconscious patterns are better handled if they are taken into awareness and their prior value recognised. Most patterns work unconsciously or semi-consciously. If you can take a little distance, and look at a normal day in your work or organisation, you'll see a multitude of patterns. Fortunately, most patterns remain unconscious: otherwise you would go crazy with the decisions and choices you would constantly have to make. Most patterns support a company and give it wings to fly. Sometimes, though, they become redundant: a pattern that was effective in the past no longer helps. In fact it becomes obstructive. It can be long and hard work to get deep-rooted patterns to surface in awareness. A constellation, however, offers a simple and efficient method. When the constellation suddenly shows you the pattern 'controlling' you, it becomes much easier to release it. Often this is all that is needed to move on, free of the pattern.

Past, present and future

Learning from the past is often a sure recipe for repeating old patterns. When we try to learn from the past, for example if we try to prevent an earlier bankruptcy happening again, unconsciously we still are connected with the patterns that have been leading to the bankruptcy. The more you want to get rid of old patterns, the more likely they will be repeated.

Accepting the past means letting go of the past. Allowing the past to be over. It means being in the here and now and being ready for something new. You cannot let go of something until you have fully taken it in, accepted it in its entirety. This creates inner space for what wants to emerge from the future into the now.

Learning from the future means constantly letting go. Especially, it means releasing images that we have created about ourselves and the future. The stronger our plans, the more difficult it becomes to see the future as it approaches. There is a lot of literature about transformation. If transformation means learning from the emerging future then, by definition, you cannot know what will emerge from the transformation process. But, in a lot of this literature, authors speak about 'transformation into a more sustainable society', and so on. But in fact these are plans. If you know in advance the new form you want to take or become, you are simply executing your plans. Letting go of these plans will create more space for transformation.

Reactivating traumas

Traumas buried, often deeply, in the genes and history of an organisation can be reactivated by a proposed change. Traumas are and look different from resistance and need a different approach. You can read more about this in the chapter called Trauma in Organisations: III.10.

Changing the goal or field of attention.

When we change our policy or strategy it is inevitable that a part of society will be excluded. The part to whom we say "*no*" or "*not any more*" might be excluded. Make sure that this part of society stays in the picture, continues to be seen and valued, even if you will not work with it in the future. Then there is less chance that the dynamic of the excluded part will turn against the organisation.

Investing time, money and energy

How much is appropriate? Sometimes less turns out to be more.

You cannot invest in only one part of a system; whatever you do has consequences for other parts of the organisation. So, which is the right place to invest?

For a director of a juice factory in Brazil, the better investment was to listen to the stories told by family members – of employees fired in a previous crisis – rather than invest millions of Reals (Brazilian currency) in the factory.

Later in the book we will talk about being stuck. It takes a lot of energy to get and stay stuck. Use this unexpected source!

> **"** *There is a lot of change already present in the air or in the field, ready to be grabbed and used. Stick your nose in the air and sniff-out what is almost here. You just need to tune in to the right wavelength!* **"**
>
> *Jan Jacob Stam*

II.3 Problems, symptoms and solutions

Organisational problems such as conflicts, losing market share, rebellion and resistance look completely different when viewed from the systemic perspective: new and different solutions pop up. The old standbys of teambuilding, going into different markets, dismissing the rebel 'leader' or breaking the resistance, just will not help here.

From the systemic perspective, problems are solutions; what is experienced as the problem in an organisation is actually the solution. It is the system reacting to violation of one of the four systemic principles. These four systemic principles, elaborated in chapter I-1 are in service of the survival of the organisational system as a whole. So the source, of what is experienced as a problem, is an attempt to ensure survival of the system. Survival on many different levels: survival of society as a whole, of the organisation or its teams and departments, or the person as part of the organisation. When we look at the problem in this way, we can discern something completely different about the problem. What is it trying to tell us about the system? Where should we look for the real causes of the problem? What interventions might produce a desired effect?

Some examples:

Co-operation

If there are conflicts in a team and the team members have willingly tried several things already but the conflict continues, then the struggle in the team often reflects an unsolved conflict elsewhere in the organisation.

For example, in a rehabilitation centre co-operation between doctors, psychologists and movement therapists remained difficult, in spite of several well-intended efforts. It appeared to be a reflection of the doubt existing in the organisation about the order of guiding principles. Are we a medical institution where the practice of medicine is the guiding principle? Or are we guided by what is best for the well being of our patients? Or is the purpose of the rehabilitation centre to get patients mobilised and out of care as quickly as possible?

Uncertainty about the order of guiding principals will inhibit collaboration and synergy in a team and even will generate conflicts between groups within the team. The lack of a clear order means that each profession (doctors, psychologists, occupational therapists, administrators and so on) is constantly, and unconsciously, looking for this order in his or her relationship with the other professions in the team. This can affect people outside of the team. For example, the social worker runs the risk of becoming the team's social worker rather than working for the patients and their families.

So we now see that the lack of cooperation is actually an expression of the lack of clear guiding principles.

Rebellion

Can rebellion also be a solution if we look at it in the right way? As a manager, I know just how uncomfortable it can be trying to handle rebellion: the feeling that your legs are being cut away from underneath you; the unexpected remarks during the team meeting that suddenly jeopardise the plan you were so pleased with. You would like to throw your 'colleagues' out of the room.

But a rebel also knows that he or she runs the risk of being expelled or fired – which often happens. Whether right or wrong, the whistle-blower often ends up without a job or the prospect of getting one again.

Somehow, rebels tend to elevate themselves to a higher position in the organisational system's hierarchy. This is uncomfortable for the managers. They feel their position is not respected by the rebel. But you might wonder why a rebel would run the risk of being fired. There must be something else: something more precious than losing one's job. (I have never seen a rebel who was driven by egotistic motives.)

When we can see them clearly, we see that they are driven by devotion to the whole system. We could even call it love for the whole system. Often a rebel is the keeper of important information about the system as a whole, information vital to the survival of the system. But if the first thing we do is reprimand the rebel, put him or her (back) in their place, then this vital information can be lost forever.

What would happen if managers first listened, really listened, to what the rebel has to say, rather than acting out of habit, fear or anger? How much courage is needed to really listen? At the very least, the courage to face the truth of what is happening in the system.

Resistance

Although change implies a future state or perspective, resistance is mostly connected with the present or the past: an intense solidarity with something that once was good or important in the organisation. Resistance tries to show that something precious has been lost or is in danger. When the agents of change are unaware of the systemic explanation, they see only people who want nothing to change, people trying to maintain the status quo. This is a superficial interpretation which, unintentionally, might well support the goals of those who are resisting.

If whatever made the organisation what it is now is not recognised, even if that has become dysfunctional, then the reaction of the system is to make employees or departments identify with that which is in danger of being lost and to fight for its survival. So we can see why they are looking to the past and why they become increasingly obstinate the more they are pushed towards the future. Be mindful that this isn't about the past being good or not good, it is about acknowledging the past in a respectful way.

Many teachers who entered the profession during the wave of democratisation in the 1960s and 1970s, brought passion and ideals for a better world and better education, and should be acknowledged for what they tried to do at and for that era. Of course they know well that today's world needs other ideals and goals, but such sincere recognition makes it much easier for them, in the here and now, to turn towards the future. It enables them to consider proposed changes in terms of their value for the present and the future, instead of unconsciously comparing them with the past.

So the main question when you are meeting resistance is: "*For whom or what are these persons, in their so called resistance, working so hard? What are they trying to protect? With what or whom are they identified? Consciously or unconsciously?*"

For what is the problem a solution?

It should now be clear that for most organisational problems of a sys-temic nature, the cause lies somewhere other than where the problem (the symptom), manifests. If a problem has been worked on several times and there is still no visible improvement, this can be seen as a strong indi-cation that something in the bigger system is the real issue.

Questions that might help to identify the root of the problem include:

- For what could this problem be a solution?
- Who or what is asking for attention via this problem?
- What pattern is being repeated here?
- Where in the organisation might this pattern belong?

One of the nice things about looking at organisational problems in this way, is that it can lead to unexpected solutions. Often many more and dif-ferent solutions than initially believed possible. There are so many ways to deal with the data that a rebel or symptom-carrier presents. And there are just as many ways to acknowledge to what these people and their (so-called) resistance are connected. We could see this as solution space appearing where previously there was only a solution. Solution space is much wider than a solution.

Systemic Intervention and Systemic Coaching

So how can we apply all this in our practice? What does it require and what skills are needed?

Systemic intervention is the art of letting co-workers, teams or deci-sion makers get a totally different perspective on an issue by offering them some appropriate questions or remarks, or simply stating clearly what you see. This moves the focus from looking for the solution to a problem, to looking for whatever it is for which the problem, itself, is the solution. This requires an inner attitude of wanting to look openly at the whole. It means letting go of assumptions and prejudices (pre-judgements), plans and cyn-icism and, moreover, not getting tangled-up in the problem yourself – be-cause then you can no longer see the wood for the trees. But it does mean to be ready to embrace the problem, to embrace the dark sides of the organisation, and not to hide from it in a solution.

So, basically, when you are looking at a problem from a systemic viewpoint, you zoom out to a larger level instead of zooming in, analysing and looking for details. It is more a stance of leaning back, exposing yourself to what the problem has to say, than interfering in the problem. It is more about hearing than listening, more about seeing than looking. There is more information in-between the words than in the words, more to learn in the not-knowing than in the knowing.

Silence, not-knowing and not-having-a-clue are the friends of the systemic manager, coach or facilitator.

Systemic intervention is also the art of doing the right thing at the right time.

Acknowledging openly what wants to be acknowledged, redressing an imbalance in giving and taking, taking a little step backwards or forwards, doing something that carries a risk, setting a remembrance stone at the entrance to the new company building and so on.

Systemic intervention does not need a constellation per se, as long as we are using systemic principles. Every owner, manager, colleague and employee can do this. In addition to the attitude we described earlier, it requires knowledge of and sensitivity to systemic principles... and the courage to test them, apply them and harvest the results. In education, in the classroom, this has been happening for some time, with often startling effects on the learning performance of the pupils and the atmosphere in the classroom. A school teacher, gently placing an empty chair for a supporting parent at the side of a child struggling with a calculation task, saw the results of the child improve dramatically.

In the organisational world, more and more managers are becoming interested in the art of systemic intervention and learning how to apply systemic intelligence when making decisions.

Systemic coaching simply means coaching from a systemic perspective. The coach stays outside the client's system. As with systemic intervention, it is about asking questions that expand and change the coachee's perspective, so that solution space suddenly appears. Therefore it is not so much about the wellbeing of the client, but about the well-being of the client's whole system. The coach can also suggest that the client imagine a constellation or, if necessary, he can use objects, perhaps on a table top, to visualise the field. Systemic coaching requires a coach with substantial doses of systemic perception and systemic sensitivity. A coach able to make use of the client's stored holographic information about the organisation as a whole. The art is to get access to that unconscious level while staying in contact with the client.

It appears that systemic coaching, observing, perceiving and intervening are, clearly, natural qualities and skills that all people have. It is nothing new. At most it is a language of cooperation, in a group or system, that has fallen out of use. But, once re-experienced it very quickly feels both natural and valuable. Anyone who wants to learn it can learn it. Experience shows that the biggest obstacles are existing patterns and prejudices.

II.4 Three consciences and four movements in life and organisations

Bert Hellinger has a particular systemic and phenomenological way of looking at families, organisations and other social systems. His ability to observe purely and without judgement has been invaluable to him (and us) and to the development of this work.

Over the years he has revealed three important mechanisms that are responsible for the way people connect themselves to systems and for the patterns appearing within those systems.

Hellinger calls these mechanisms 'consciences', a term that, perhaps, could have been chosen more appropriately, because the word 'conscience' already evokes so many existing associations. A number of books have been published that are devoted entirely to these consciences. So we'll just take a brief look.

The Personal Conscience

When you are doing anything, personal conscience lets you know, immediately, if your actions make you belong less or more to a group, family, organisation or system. Think of the organisation where you work at the moment. What behaviour makes you feel you belong to it more and what behaviour makes you run the risk of being ejected. Think of an association or club, of which you are a member, and ask yourself the same question *"What would I have to do here for them to give me the cold shoulder?"* Think of your country or your religion and ask the same question. Often these rules can be found in codes of conduct or employee handbooks, or just look at what your organisation considers are reasons for instant dismissal. These make it clear to you when you have crossed the border of the personal conscience of the organisation.

As a junior advisor in my first job, in a district water board in the Netherlands, I was urged to speak with a clear 'g'. (Pronunciation of the characteristic Dutch 'g' has strong regional differences). If I didn't, they would immediately know that I was not speaking 'their' language and then it would be difficult to be accepted by them.

Once, as a consultant, I almost lost an interim assignment in Friesland (a province in the north), when the clients realised that I didn't speak Frisian, the local dialect. I knew I was in trouble but, luckily, I mentioned that my mother is a Halbertsma (a well-known Frisian name) from Grou (a town in Friesland). *"Oh! You should have said that before"* was the reaction. Roughly translated this meant, *"You're alright after all. Now you belong; you are one of us"*.

Personal conscience is also the conscience of good and bad, of right and wrong. Good is when you do something and you experience the inner feeling that people are smiling or looking happily at you.. Bad is that which does not fit within the boundaries that shape the conscience of the group. The stronger the identity of a group, the stronger the boundaries are and the easier it is to exclude.

Be careful though... this conscience does not care, objectively, if you do the most horrible things: a suicide attack in Afghanistan brings the perpetrator closer to his people or his group; killing North Vietnamese civilians made you a good American; certain believers are allowed to defend and spread their religions by fire and sword, and damaging a competitor enhances your position as sales director. All these things are done with a good conscience.

The Collective Conscience

The second conscience guards the survival of the system as a whole. The collective conscience, as Hellinger calls it, is in fact the system's conscience. Unlike the personal conscience, it works unconsciously.

If a founder of a successful company is not remembered and respected, even if this is unintentional, then the collective conscience makes sure that groups of co-workers, even those joining the organisation long after the founder has left the company, become identified with the founder or his ideas. These workers do not consciously pursue this identification or know that it is happening to them. It might be seen, for example, as sudden and inexplicable resistance from the workforce to changes proposed by the current management.

Also forms of burnout, whereby someone unconsciously tries to fulfil somebody else's tasks in addition to their own, is an act of the collective conscience. If you, unconsciously, have the tendency to fulfil someone else's responsibilities, you have no reference for when the job is done. When you are doing your own job, you know when it is done. When you do someone else's job, you don't. Your body will stop you with a burn-out or heart-attack.

Aspects of the glass ceiling, whereby a woman withdraws inwardly at his or her nomination for the most senior position, is also an example of how the collective conscience works. This example is elaborated in chapter III-5

An individual, or even a whole department, can become unconsciously entangled in the system. To put it in other ways, the collective conscience has taken into service a person or part of the organisation in order to prevent an important element being excluded, or that groups of people must pay a high price for the wealth and success of the organisation or that the natural order in the system is turned upside down.

We will give examples, in several places, of how the collective conscience works in organisations, because, once you can recognise it, you can manage it. Much of the dysfunction in organisations has its origins in the working of the collective conscience, as do repeating patterns or examples of unwanted outcomes.

The Spirit-mind

The third conscience is a universal conscience. It is a mechanism with a creative force and direction and it considers all systems and all people to be of equal value. Hellinger calls this mechanism 'spirit-mind'. This conscience transcends the personal and collective consciences. It also transcends the judgements of good and bad or right and wrong. This is the conscience that makes reconciliation possible and leads to inner rest. When an organisation is in resonance with this conscience, the organisation is firmly rooted in reality and is in contact with its destiny in society. This conscience enables organisations or individuals to accept the world as it is, with each element standing in its full power. The organisation lets itself be taken into service by its destiny. And sometimes this can mean that the organisation is limited in some way. Marketing in resonance with this conscience means that the organisation totally reveals itself to society and wonders, 'What is society trying to tell us?'

Like the 'first', this conscience is also immediately perceptible. You can feel when you are in resonance with your destiny or an organisation is in resonance with its destiny. You notice that you are allowing the spirit-mind to take you into whatever service it deems right for you (or the organisation). You can also feel very easily when you do not act in resonance with this conscience: unrest and inner doubt arise. The wisdom of knowing what works and does not work indicates resonance with the spirit-mind.

You can see all three of these consciences as fields: fields that bring you into motion, fields that immobilise you, fields that give an organisation wings and so on. As you begin to become more familiar with them, you'll also notice that they can often interact with and against one another.

Lets look at what happens when an employee in a nursing home is found to be mistreating residents. He is fired, immediately. What happened is forgotten as quickly as possible, kept out of the press and covered-up. This very understandable reaction comes from the first conscience: the perpetrator no longer belongs to the system (the nursing home) and neither do the things he or she did to the residents.

But some years later a newly-appointed psychologist senses a very heavy atmosphere in one of the teams and she feels she cannot do her work properly. She enquires but is met with a shrug of the shoulders. However, through some persistent questioning she discovers what happened some time ago. In a constellation it becomes clear that a part of the team feels victimised: they are unconsciously identified with the victims who, at the time, were also excluded. Another part of the team is easily angered: they are unconsciously identified with the perpetrator and the excluded perpetrator-energy. So the second (the collective) conscience tried to give both the perpetrator and the victim a place again in the system, by taking into service groups of employees to represent perpetrator-energy and victim-energy.

Four movements

The three consciences, the personal conscience, the collective conscience and spirit-mind, are three different mechanisms or layers that determine how it feels and how it goes in a system: family, organisational or social. You can also see them as three fields; once you have had personal experience of each of the three fields, you will notice that the movements you tend to make or to follow in each field, are different. Different in nature, different in direction and bringing different outcomes to the actions you take and the decisions you make.

The movements in the fields of these three consciences are quite different in nature, but they are all there. In addition there is still a fourth movement, the one of autopoiesis, that is just a bit separate from the other three. Autopoiesis, self-creation, is the movement where a system itself mobilises the necessary resources to overcome a problem or not-desired state.

An example

During our six-month sabbatical together, our big play-time, my wife and I were consciously experiencing these four movements and experimenting with what would happen if we were to follow one movement or another.

The first movement of the personal conscience is characterised, above all, by following what you want. It is the movement of the will. It appeals to your thinking, your mind and your wishes. It is the movement of setting out a strategy, a plan and goals. Sometimes a plan takes us across the borders of the personal conscience, to where we can feel that there is risk, and we are curious about 'how might this harm me?' For example, we want to tap into a new market because, to us, this seems fun and worthwhile and we would become better than our competitors. There are also feelings of fear about what will happen when we go into new territory, when we cross the boundaries of the familiar ground of the personal conscience. These movements are well known in the world of entrepreneurship and management.

Personally, I know this movement very well. I am good at planning and if someone asks me what I feel like or what I want to do, then I'm rarely short of answers. Bibi, my wife, is much less familiar with these inner movements. If you ask her what she wants to do in her sabbatical, ideas don't immediately start flowing. It is not that she doesn't want anything, it's just a movement with which she is less familiar. Naturally, that regularly leads to despair, incomprehension and conflicts in our relationship and our professional life. But the tranquillity of our sabbatical helped us to learn much more about this.

The second movement follows the collective conscience. Do what the system asks you to do, for which you were taken into service. These are also precisely the unconscious patterns and entanglements from which you then start to act. Someone who is unconsciously trying to fulfil another person's task, will go to work feeling a sense of responsibility that something has to be finished. A mother's son (like me) will have a tendency to try to save the earth (the earth is the equivalent of mother). My wife who, for a long time in her life, unconsciously lived the life of her dead brother, does not know very well what she wants for herself. However, she can feel, very well, what others want and is driven to fulfil that, even if it means that she must put her own needs and wants aside.

So if you ask me "What must you do today?", *immediately in me there is an* "Oops, don't come too close with this question. I do not want to become too entangled in a system". *When you ask the same question to my wife, she has already acted before she can think about the possible answers.*

The third movement follows the spirit-mind conscience. Moving in resonance with your destiny, beyond good and bad or right and wrong, and also beyond the systems of which you are a part: your family, your work, your country or culture. You let yourself be taken into service by something bigger. Something beyond even ideals. This does not mean running an environmentally-responsibility business because it looks good and makes you feel good (that is the first conscience). Neither does it mean doing so because you want to save the earth because 'she' cannot do it herself (that is the second conscience). It means running an environmentally-responsible business because you simply have to, because you feel you have no choice, because you feel it is right.

For me, following this third movement during our sabbatical meant, for example, that I left a mountain hut in the morning, with my paraglider, clothes and all I needed on my back without any plan or idea where to go. Then I started walking, letting my body decide at crossroads which direction to take, and noticed suddenly that I was climbing to a mountain plateau where the French Resistance had gathered during the Second World War. There I stayed for the day, noticing how I let my body guide me to memorials and special places. The next day I climbed to a mountain pass, spread my canopy and flew where the wind would carry me.

Bibi could also follow this movement well, and to our surprise we found we could also follow this movement well together. In the mornings we would wake and carry this question lightly within us, "What draws us now?" And then, as we followed this golden thread, we found ourselves suddenly on the top of a mountain in Ireland. We could never have imagined, only a few hours earlier, that we would be there. And there wasn't even a path to the top. But suddenly we were there, in harmony, in resonance, full of life and peaceful at the same time.

Acting in accordance with the movement of the spirit-mind gives a great inner peace and a knowing – without knowing consciously.

The fourth movement is the one of autopoiesis, originally a form of constellation developed by Siegfried Essen. Autopoiesis means auto creating. The underlying notion is an awareness that each system is capable of mobilising the movements and resources that lead to its fulfilment. The invitation to this movement could be, "You are free, really free, to do all that is needed to find a place in this system that is good for yourself and good for the whole". This movement also mobilises your sense of responsibility to find your own right place and a place for the others in a system. Repetition of 'free, really free…' reminds you that you can and may act beyond the borders of the first and second conscience, in order to mobilise, for example, those resources that are needed from outside the system.

Banks

Holland is in a banking-crisis. Recently I decided, in a split second, not to leave the big bank where I am a customer – as long I keep putting money in that bank. (This act-in-an-instant decision is in accordance with the spirit-mind). Then, a few days later, I wrote a letter to the CEO of this bank, describing my decision not to leave and go to a more sustainable smaller bank. I told them that from my viewpoint we all co-created this crisis, and leaving or blaming the bank would not be of any help. I wrote that I wanted to talk to the CEO of 'my bank', in order to ask him, face-to-face: "What can I do and what can you do to restore trust in banking. Your problem is also my problem. I want to face the fact that I am also a part of the problem and act from there". *This is an example of an autopoietic movement. To my pleasant surprise I got many phone calls from the bank, inviting me to go into the discussion I raised. The tone of these phone calls was surprising. They were not to defend the bank, they were not coming from the usual 'PR-machine', as the bank-man told me. (Meaning:* "Our reaction is not coming from the collective conscience, or from the usual patterns"). *How this will continue, I will let you know in my next book, probably about systemic work and societal issues.*

How can you work with this now?

First of all you can just feel if you recognise the movements. Just take a dilemma, something where you are stuck: in your life, your work or your organisation. Then feel, one by one, to where each movement leads. Feel how you start moving and to where, when you ask yourself "*What do I want?*". This is a question that invokes actions from the first, the personal conscience.

Where do I arrive when I follow the patterns and scripts of my life? This is a question to invoke actions from the second, the collective conscience.

To where am I drawn if I let myself being taken by a bigger force? Following the call of the conscience of the spirit-mind.

What must I do when I take my responsibility to find a right place for myself, in and for the other people, the family members, the organisation and the world to which I belong?

Many people who do this exercise say that it makes them really aware of the, often, conflicting movements with which they struggle. Just noticing this immediately increases the available solution space.

You can also ask yourself which of these four movements are more familiar to you and what might new movements be and feel like. Or what would be a good balance of the four movements for you, at this moment, in your (professional) life.

When I came back from my sabbatical it was fine for me to go to work again. But being back in harness again, answering to my agenda and my institute, really stressed me out. For a while I seriously considered cancelling all my appointments, all the workshops and training courses that were planned for the coming fifteen months and withdrawing from the Bert Hellinger Institute in order to follow, exclusively, the movements of the spirit and to see what would arise. But the movement of autopoiesis caught hold of me: my sense of responsibility for finding a good place for myself and the others urged me first to make sure that our institute and our co-workers would be in good hands. I started looking for resources. Actually they were as plentiful as blackberries in summer, because within a week two new trainers presented themselves, and one of them also had managerial qualities and wanted to take on this role. So, finally, a new balance in these four movements is being formed, a balance that leads to anchoring, deepening and growth and to new, still unknown, fields.

Try imagining:

- How would a management team meeting look if it was conducted mostly in the spirit of the first movement?
- How would it look in the spirit of the second movement?

- How would it look if the team meeting followed the third movement?

- What would you hear if you attended a directors meeting taking place in service of the fourth movement?

Take a look around you, do you recognise organisations that, especially, follow the first movement, or the second movement, or are in service of the third movement, or seem to find the fourth movement the most important?

II.5 Organisations from the perspective of the spirit-mind

Whenever something is built or constructed, like a building, city or society, it has the natural tendency, eventually, to decline or decay. This precisely follows the second law of thermodynamics. Energy has the natural tendency to find its lowest form: heat. Producing electricity requires a lot of energy; finally it always declines back into heat. As long as we conduct regular maintenance, what we build remains intact.

But what happens to the creations of the force known as spirit-mind? Spirit-mind is an evolutionary force, stimulating the larger and smaller transitions of and in the world. Spirit-mind is capable of bringing in the kind of impulse, from outside a system, needed to break repeating patterns in that system.

Spirit-mind is also beyond good, bad, right and wrong. It looks favourably upon everyone and everything in the world, war and destruction included. Spirit-mind is beyond the will, plans and control of human beings, although it can align with them all beautifully. Spirit-mind develops as it develops itself, sometimes with a great deal of force and violence. When the crust of the earth creased and mountains appeared, gigantic forces must have been at work. The forces that caused the migration of people around the earth must have been enormous. In practice it might have looked like they were searching for new territories and food, but the urge to discover, to cross oceans, to travel to the moon must have been stimulated by a huge force field. Apparently all kinds of things on this earth want to develop, whether we like it or not. When Otto Scharmer, and the philosophers upon whom his thinking is based, talk about the emerging future, the future as it approaches us, they are talking about this force. It is not only a force of beginnings, of growth and evolution, it is also a force of destruction, decline and death. This force begins life cycles and ends life cycles; short life cycles and long life cycles. The energy for these life cycles comes from… *"Yes! From where actually?"* Almost effortlessly these cycles are generated as if they are in contact with, and are fed by, vast energy sources. Energy that seems to be freely available to them.

Our son has the ability to be in the right place, at the right time, with the right people. He experiences this as something natural; he is neither proud of it nor does he use it inappropriately. He does not feel the need to apply for new jobs: he trusts that they will come to him in the natural flow of life. This doesn't take him out of contact with society; on the contrary, it brings him into a deeper contact. I was rather shocked when, upon asking him about his ideals, he told me he had none. As a child of the 1960s, at his age I was full of ideals and ideas about how we could shape and reshape society. On the other hand our son does not know what practising is: his experience is that you can either do something or you cannot. As a child he tried, once a year, to ride a bike. If he fell off, no problem, he would try again the following year.

It's a totally different story with our daughter: she is very good at practising. She can put a lot of energy into mastering something: endless repetition, working very hard to get the right results… and she gets them! Her world looks tidy and orderly. She is good at what she does and is constantly improving. She is proud of what she achieves, although, like her brother, she does not boast about it. She will persevere through difficult situations and rise from them. She likes exploring things that no one else has explored. Others seem to notice her attitude and approach, as she has been offered a complex PhD position researching biological pest control. PhD research and blood, sweat and tears go together. Or, in other words, they both need the kind of energy that moves mountains.

We can see a kind of parallel to this brother and sister story in two of the ways organisations are formed:

- The first one is: you can build-up or construct an organisation. This needs a lot of energy; not only to build it but also to maintain it. Many organisations are built by willpower, starting from an idea about what is possible or needed in society. The reconstruction of Europe, following the Second World War, is an example: huge effort and enormous sums of money from abroad made it possible. Or look at the incredible amount of land the Dutch have reclaimed from the sea and the Delta Works sea-defences they built to protect their land and people. Sweat is still dripping from these works, they still inspire awe. And the companies that built the dykes and sluices to control the water were also, in a way, built by the process. The same is true for the VOC (The Dutch East-India Company), the first multinational Dutch business, founded in the seventeenth century to exploit the rich natural resources of the Far East and bring them to Europe.

- The second approach is to let an organization emerge. An organisation can be created in resonance with the spirit-mind. It is a natural process, fed from a seemingly invisible and infinite source of energy. The organisation grows as it wants to grow, in harmonious balance with the surrounding world. Society changes, so the organisation changes in a natural response. When the organisation reaches its destiny it ends its existence.

Marketing, in a constructed organisation, via the will, means creating a new product and taking it to market... taking it to market. This costs a lot of energy.

Marketing from the spirit-mind means being open to everything society is constantly broadcasting, and always asking *"What is society trying to tell our organisation?"*.

Leading an organisation from building-up is taking the organisation by the hand. Leading an organisation from the spirit-mind is letting yourself be taken by the hands of the organisation and society.

Acting from building-up is executing a plan. Acting from the spirit-mind often means acting on the spur on the moment, before your neurones are engaged. The movement comes much more from the body than the brain.

In downsizing, or even when an end seems inevitable, we can still put a lot of energy into keeping an organisation going or revitalising it. But we do have a choice: we can also accept and respect the natural movement and use the energy released, by downsizing or death, for something new.

Building-up and the will always try to combat illness in an organisation. Spirit-mind accepts illness as belonging to life and development, and opens up to the message illness carries about the organisation as a whole. Then spirit-mind acts.

From the will we develop a mission for the organisation. From spirit-mind we are led by guiding principals that are already present in the organisation.

And, from the spirit-mind perspective, what is sustainability and working sustainably? We could spend our energy imagining a new form of society: we all know something has to change in the world. But, we can also take the world as it is and tune in to the ripples of change as they first appear.

Building and changing from the perspective of feasibility, will and construction takes a lot of energy.

Building and changing from spirit-mind requires a sense of marvel, of wonder and of admiration for what wants to develop.

Admiration is an active process. By admiring something we encourage it to continue developing, irrespective of whether we know exactly what is developing and in what direction it will go. So, we can admire the next generation, who think in ways we don't understand and, perhaps, never will. Through admiring we contribute our focused attention (energy) to something new and, consequently, the new development has a greater chance to thrive.

Marvelling is the process where we create an inner space for something new, something we do not yet know, something we will never find with our old familiar ways of thinking. Something that is here and now, wants to appear or to make its own movement. Marvelling is also being open to learning and developing from the future as it comes towards us. Besides needing the quality of presencing, marvelling also requires the courage to let go: to release old patterns and make space for new, sometimes unexpected, patterns. Space for ideas that want to crystallize and seeds that want to grow... in their own directions.

Most of you will already have realised that the spirit-mind accepts both forms of organisational development: its 'own' and that of building-up and will.

II.6 Organisational constellations: methods, conditions and reflections

Although this book is not about the phenomenon of systems constellations, we cannot ignore it. In this chapter we'll look briefly at constellations, what they are and how they go and then we'll reflect a little about them.

In a constellation the following happens: the issue holder determines, in consultation with the facilitator of the constellation, what elements are needed to picture the organisational question of the issue holder. For example, a shop owner wants to know if there is anything else that might be playing a part in his issue of his inability to find a buyer for his shop. The elements, to begin with, would be the shop (S), the owner (O) – who, in this case, is also the issue holder – and the potential buyers (PBs).

From the participants in the workshop the issue holder chooses one person to represent each element. The representatives know nothing more about the case than what they heard in the initial consultation. The issue holder places the representatives in the working space, in relation to each other, or the representatives are directed to find their own places, again in relation to each other. Something astounding then happens: the representatives experience the same perceptions, feelings and tendencies as the real 'elements' in the actual organisation. How this works we do not yet know. Of course we check with the issue holder if the constellation corresponds sufficiently to the real organisation. Only about ten times, in the two thousand or so constellations I have facilitated, has an issue holder not recognised 'their' constellation.

Then, depending on the question, we can apply interventions within the constellation. Interventions are tests aimed at finding out the underlying reason why the situation in the organisation is the way it is. Put systemically... for what is the symptom (not being able to sell the shop) a solution?

In this approach we work on the assumption that when unconscious patterns become visible they are easier to handle and they offer the issue holder more possibilities for action. A constellation is never a command about what must be done: it is the issue holder who makes this decision.

It is the facilitator who suggests certain tests or movements – the interventions; but only if the issue holder agrees. Then a subtle dance develops involving the issue holder, the constellation and the facilitator.

In the example, the PBs' representative approaches the field (space) where S and O have been set up (placed), but he stops. He hesitates, as if in front of an invisible door. S withdraws until his back is literally against one of the walls. O is looking between S and the PBs to a point somewhere in the distance.

The first test the facilitator suggests is to bring in the original guiding principle of the actual shop owner (OGP). Why does the facilitator suggest this test when there are so many possibilities? Because the issue holder, while bringing in his question, often mentioned how his heart is no longer in the business and how the market has become one marked by distrust and deception. It is the systemic attention of the facilitator that fished this element out from the short introductory conversation.

The issue holder chooses a representative for the OGP, who is then asked to find (what feels like) a good place in the constellation. The moment the OGP comes in, the representatives of the owner and of the shop start moving and, quite quickly, the three of them form a tight cluster. PB is still in his place, but looking very closely at the cluster of three.

The next test is to set up the guiding principle of the buyers (BGP). This principle is something like Business is a game where you are allowed to trick and cheat each other. Why this test? Partly it is a logical step: to investigate the extent to which the guiding principle of the seller is compatible with the guiding principles of the buyers and if this influences the saleability of the shop. And partly this step comes from the experience-based intuition and perception of the facilitator.

The BGP slowly walks past the PBs to the cluster of S, O and OGP. The cluster elements express that they feel threatened.

Now the issue holder, who has been watching, mesmerised, suddenly lets us know that it has become painfully clear what the real issues are. He says he is now facing a choice that he finds difficult. He wants to sell his company and realises this probably means sacrificing his guiding principles. Is he ready to do this? The possibilities now come thick and fast: not selling; winding-up the company – so protecting his guiding principle; imposing conditions for guiding principles on the buyer; making buyers explain their own guiding principles and so on. What the owner actually chooses to do is not up to the constellation or the facilitator. The forces affecting the sale of this, once so successful, company have become clear to the owner. As have the consequences of the different options. But the choice is his and his alone.

At the end of the process the issue holder thanks the representatives. The facilitator emphasises that the representatives can and should now come out of their roles. Someone who represents for the first time can find the process of representing a little strange (I remember wanting to embrace another representative, without being able to explain why. I was unsure if this was something from the constellation or something from myself…) But representing can also feel quite natural.

Reflections

For those who do not know constellations I hope I have given an insight into how they work. If you tend to think more in technical terms, you can consider constellations to be a method or a technology.

But you can also see a constellation as a phenomenon (from the Greek φαινομενον, which means 'things appearing in view'). A phenomenon displaying similar qualities to phenomena that are seen and proven in the science of quantum physics, such as the phenomenon of non-locality: energy is capable of occupying different positions in space simultaneously. A constellation is a form or image of the real organisation, occurring simultaneously to that of the real organisation, but in a completely different location. Although constellations are almost always very clear, they tend not to be precise. The physician Werner Heisenberg demonstrated, in 1927, with his uncertainty principle, that the opposite of clarity is accuracy: the more you accurately you try to pin down a particle, the more it tends to escape, and then clarity gets lost. In this way constellations remind us of Heisenberg's uncertainty principle… you can never know everything about a subatomic particle. Constellations provide clear, but not very detailed information.

Fields

Albrecht Mahr, a doctor of medicine from Würzberg in Germany and one of the pioneers in the field of family constellations about illness and health, and later in the field of questions about social conflicts and war and peace, was the first to use the name The Knowing Field. He used this term to describe the phenomenon whereby representatives, who are set up in relation to one another, know information about the actual family or organisational system without having any prior knowledge of the family, organisation or information. A person (as representative), when placed in such a field, is able to sense and report what her or his corresponding element experiences in the real system.

Otto Scharmer once asked me, while we were walking through Boston, what is the minimum needed for the process we now call a constellation to take place. *"Apparently something is needed"* he insisted, *"because, otherwise, such processes would happen spontaneously in organisations"*. Although professor Matthias Varga von Kibéd presumes that constellations often do exist spontaneously as natural processes, I think there are still certain conditions, or at least elements, beneficial to stimulating the process of a constellation.

A field is needed.

Perhaps there is always a field but, just like clearing a dance floor, it is good to create such a field consciously. Just focusing attention on making such a field already works very well. Sitting in a circle seems to automatically make the encircled space into a knowing field. But when participants sit behind tables the field doesn't form.

Attention and intention

A systemic field has no judgements or opinions. It is also a field where sensations and emotions often flow freely. It helps if the people present at a constellation do not have an opinion about the issue in question. As a facilitator, one of the fastest ways I know to create the right setting for a constellation is to welcome all the people in the room, exactly as they are. Consciously including the whole background of their culture, organisations, training and the ancestors they bring along. The more their backgrounds are allowed just to be there, the stronger the field. It seems that if all the participants are allowed to be there – as they are – it becomes easier to have no judgements in the field. The more open-hearted the people present, the easier it becomes for sensations, feelings and emotions to be visible and expressed. Having an open heart means being able to listen from the place of the other. Why would someone close his or her heart? Mostly to avoid being offended or hurt again. We succeed in creating a field with an open heart when we welcome all the people present, with all their wounds healed or not healed. (This does not need to be spoken out: holding the intention is already enough).

Holding space

A host is needed. Someone who helps create the holding space and invites the field in to it. It still seems to help if this is done explicitly, but we are also seeing that, in groups that know constellations well, forming the minimum setting for a constellation often takes place spontaneously. In this case the participants create the holding space. It helps if the host or hostess indicates clearly when each constellation ends, as participants can sometimes, unintentionally, stay in their representative roles.

An issue

A theme, question or issue is needed. Constellations always need a substantive theme around which to materialise. At least one participant (It can also be a management team or a group of people) must be strongly connected with the issue and must feel connected to it. It is remarkable that it is not necessary for the representatives, or the workshop partic-

ipants, to know anything about the issue. The more the theme is connected with the 'emerging future' manifesting in the here and now, the
more force and focus there is in the constellation.

Intervention

During the process of a constellation at least one intervention is usually
needed to clarify an existing pattern or to change that pattern. Over many
years we've seen that constellations highlight the way in which patterns
keep repeating themselves in a system, until an intervention, from the
outside, brings an insight or change. For a long time it was thought that
the impulse had to come from the facilitator. But gradually it is becoming clear that it can also come from one of the participants, not necessarily a representative. It can even come from something that is outside the
field of the constellation. In the example of the constellation at MIT with
Arawana Hayashi, Otto Scharmer, me and the others, the representative
of the 'emerging future' saw something happen from the corner of her eye
outside on the street. Whatever this was, the movement outside the win-
dow somehow triggered a whole cascade of actions in the constellation.
As we backtracked later, we saw that this was the point where a shift in
the constellation started, ultimately changing the role of many elements
(like the banks, government and so on) in society. This impulse from outside, is the most unknown part of the constellation process. From where,
exactly, does the intervention come? Many experiments and observations
are under way that we hope will answer this question.

Constellations and systemic principles

Here I want to differentiate between the constellations method and systemic principles. Over time, the constellations method and systemic principles have become interwoven. But they don't have to stay interwoven
under all circumstances. What you use, and how, depends above all on
the question or issue at hand.

The development of constellations owes much to the German therapist, philosopher and ex-priest Bert Hellinger. Since around 1990 he has
been using constellations for family systems, organisational systems and

bigger social systems. Hellinger has also constantly used the constellations to investigate the nature of social systems, what their binding principles are and how patterns, constructive and destructive, originate and develop. Thanks to his investigative attitude we now have a treasure chest of systemic principles – a constantly expanding systemic knowledge base!

These systemic principles are the main subject of this book. It appears that once you have mastered the systemic principles (have found your own combination of knowledge, understanding and sensing) you do not always need the constellations method to get a systemic view of organisational development. The purpose of this book is to invite you to put on your systemic 'glasses' and to look at organisations from a very different perspective.

The power of constellations

Looking back at what I have just written you could almost believe that organisational constellations are slowly giving way to a constellation-free systemic perspective on organisational questions. Working without constellations certainly seems very attractive: you don't need a facilitator, nor would you have all the fuss and bother involved in assembling enough representatives and finding an appropriate space.

But… besides the help they give to every issue holder, constellations are an unbelievably rich source of insight about everyday phenomena in organisations. I would never have discovered the concept of guiding principles (as a way of understanding what was going on in particular organisations) had I not facilitated constellations in which current knowledge and thinking appeared not to work. By facilitating many constellations about brand issues the systemic nature of brands emerged, as well as the insight that a problematic relationship between brand and market often reflects an unsolved conflict or pattern within the organisation. Run a day of constellations about investments and the systemic principles around investments start emerging. We do not construct those principles. They emerge as phenomena and show themselves to the attentive observer.

Using only the tools of systemic observations, interventions and conversations, we would not have discovered most of those principles. So it is fair to presume that constellations will be with us for a long time.

II.7 Organisation: field or structure?

Seldom has such a small, simple thing influenced my thinking about organisations as much as the drawing Thomas Latka [1] made on a flip chart one Sunday morning.

Structure of field

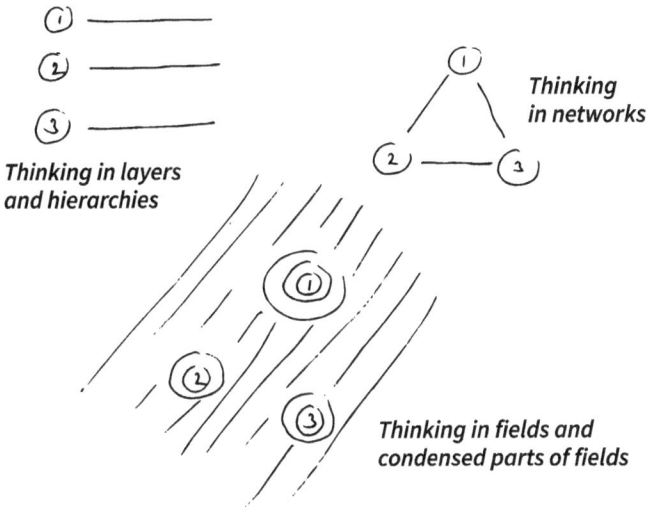

Our small group of colleagues, from different countries, are together in the Dolomites for our annual Systemic Think Tank, where we exchange, experiment and co-create around the phenomenon of systemic work in organisations. New approaches are always welcome and this year we embrace Theory U and Presencing as well as other systemic approaches such as those of Jean Paul Rességuier's 'physiotherapy'.

And the following idea starts presenting itself... that you can consider organisations as both structures and fields, just as light can be particles

---

[1] Thomas is a philosopher in the art of topology. Topology (from the Greek τοπος ,'place', and λογος ,'study') is the mathematical study of shapes and spaces.

and waves. Both are true, both are useful.

The organisation as a field

When you consider an organisation as a field, the elements of the organisation – the departments, the products, the services, the people – make up the density of this field. In the spaces between the elements is at least as much information as in the elements, as quantum physics has already proved. Each member of any system has information about the whole system. Constellations have shown this thousands of times, even if we do not yet know how it happens. Each element (representative) is just like a hologram, storing all the information about the whole picture. If you think of the hologram as a transparent film similar to (old) photo negatives, and you tear it into two pieces, both pieces will show the whole picture. If you tear it in half again, all four pieces will show the complete image. As you tear again, the image stays complete but it becomes, little by little, less clear.

In an organisation this hologram phenomenon is even more remarkable than in a family. In a family you might think that it is 'something in the genes' that allows each family member to know about the system as a whole. This applies even to previously 'unknown' family members who only come to light during the constellation: members who might have been ignored, perhaps because they were part of a shameful family secret hushed-up for generations. All family members have the ability to perceive the whole system.

In organisations you don't have biological genes. You can't choose to be a part of your family – you are born into it. But you can choose to take part in an organisation voluntarily; at least that is what we like to believe. How is it possible that people, as soon as they become part of an organisational system, seem, almost magically, to have unconsciously-stored information about the whole? Where lies the consciousness of a person? In his or her body or in a larger field around it? Where lies the consciousness of an organisation? In the members or in the spaces between them? Where does a good idea come from in a group in that is presencing? Usually it is an individual who verbalises the idea, but it seems to come through them rather than from them. 'Listening from the field', Otto Scharmer and his colleagues call it.

The biologist Rupert Sheldrake conducted many experiments, during the latter half of the last century, some very simple and replicable, that led him to develop the concept of morphic fields. A characteristic of morphic fields is that patterns within these fields tend to repeat themselves. A striking example came out of his research into accident 'black spots' in England. Black spots are places where, without apparent reasons, many more traffic accidents occur than the national average. Sheldrake discovered that those black spots were mostly sites of former battlefields.

The historian, Anne-Encelin Schûtzenberger, researched repeating traumatic events in, for example, royal families. She found that events repeated on exactly the same dates, while it was impossible for the people involved to have known about any previous traumatic events. Anngwyn St. Just found something similar in her research on the repetition of traffic accidents and other traumatic events.

Bert Hellinger, the father of systemic work, also went through a similar development. When he began his Systemische Familientherapie he considered the family as a structure and the members as elements forming that structure and his initial constellations were, mainly, static. Slowly it became clear to him, via his phenomenological perspective on the world, that we all are fields of consciousness. Families and their members, organisations, social systems are all fields nested within greater fields. Nowadays, Hellinger's constellations are very condensed: he does not set up the members of a system in relation to each other (the classic constellation), but sets up only one or two representatives, in relation to the field.

A big advantage of considering organisations and other living systems as fields is that a field also has a direction, and movements within that field also have (their own) directions. As a chemist friend put it "*Oh, you mean something like a vector diagram*". A vector diagram is a visual representation of the magnitude and direction of forces (in a system), indicated by the use of arrows. The force lines of a vector diagram are not necessarily coupled to the elements involved, they can also go through the space between the elements.

Sheldrake had already found that 'his' morphic fields tended to repeat patterns. Change seems to need an impulse from outside the system. Bert Hellinger distinguishes three different kind of consciences; we could call them the binding forces in organisations. The first conscience tells you if your behaviour takes you further into the group or takes you further out of the group. The second conscience repeats patterns, unconsciously, in order to secure the survival of a system as a whole. The third conscience is a creating conscience; it has a direction and is a kind of evolutionary force capable of breaking the repetition of patterns. Otto Scharmer speaks, in the context of learning organisations, of the danger inherent in learning from the past: there is a significant chance that the old patterns will simply find us again. Learning from the future is a way, perhaps, of letting ourselves be found by new, previously unknown patterns.

And what does that mean for working with organisations now?

Without being able to explain it, thinking-in-fields for organisations seems to be an exciting approach, an addition that offers new points of view and new kinds of interventions. Of course the effects of this way of looking at organisations need to be tested on their merits.

An example from the 'field' of constellators that shows how organising by structure fails: In the greater world of systemic work, across all the fields of families, organisations, education, illness/health and society, an interesting, maybe puzzling, phenomenon is visible. Thousands of professionals, all over the world, are at work opening up this way of systemic working: applying it, investigating it and developing it. There is a strong urge to meet: to exchange insights, to train, to redefine – just as in any developing science. I am lucky to be invited to practise this work in about twenty different countries, over several continents. As soon a professional association, foundation or other structure for systemic work is formed, irrespective of the country, the energy seems to flow out of it. After a joyful, enthusiastic and energetic beginning, the organisations suffer a moribund existence. The development of the work seems to progress in spite of these organisations rather than because of them. I can think of just one country where such an organisation is a bit more viable, thanks to the personal efforts of a widely-respected person who has invested a lot of personal energy into it.

But if you consider systemic work as a field and its professionals, whether or not with their own organisations, as concentrations of the field's energy, then, suddenly, you can see that real development becomes possible. Someone in that field is moved to organise a congress for professional exchange and professionals pour in, attracted by the energy in the idea. They meet, just as they are, and precisely where each one is in their field and their development. Smaller fields meet, bigger fields form and then the greater field starts flowing. Co-creation arises. After two days everybody goes their own way, surrounded and carried by a rich field, and tries out, develops, tests… In this way the whole field is lifted and nourished. Some time later, somebody else has an idea that attracts, and crystallises as another co-creation event.

So, in the world of constellators, a successful form for organising and developing is to not get caught up in organisations with rules, standards and organisational charts. Nor in networks. Maybe the words 'social movement' are closer to describing how constellators are organised.

Many people, in times of crisis, pose the question of whether certain well-known organisational structures have come to the end of their time. It would be interesting to think more about organisations in terms of fields, and it might be surprising to see which forms arise from there.

What actually changes in organisational change? Is it the field, the structure or the 'inner space from which we operate'? (Scharmer)

When you look at organisations as fields, quite a few other questions arise.

What inner movement is there in the system? How strong is the field of repeating patterns? Can the organisation reach its destiny? From where, in the field, does the impulse originate to change a pattern?

The organisation as structure

When, from a systemic perspective, you see the organisation as a structure, an enormous number of meaningful and fascinating observations can be made. These arise out of certain characteristics of organisational systems: that they cannot stop wanting to be complete, wanting to exchange and wanting to have an internal stability that is nourished and supported by order. We devote several chapters of this book to this issue.

II.8 Innovation, Theory U and systemic phenomenological work

Otto Scharmer, who co-authored Presence with Peter Senge et al., and is a senior lecturer at MIT, interviewed more than hundred people, from all over the world who are in the middle of implementing innovation processes. What seemed remarkable was that all these people appeared to endure a similar process. At some point they all got stuck in a no-longer-functioning reality, went into a deep process of inner transformation, allowed new thinking to crystallise and then made it real, concrete. Otto named this process 'U', after the shape of the letter, as it symbolises the journey 'down into the depths and up again'.

What Scharmer's interviews did was take him along a phenomenological path, in a manner comparable to the way Hellinger came to his insights into the functioning of social systems. So we see that these theories are not about constructing a 'new' reality, but allowing an image to emerge of reality as it really is. This is just one of the many places where systemic work and Theory U fit so well together.

Before describing the U-process, I want to tell you about some of the brilliant discoveries to be found within Theory U. Where does true change originate? (Here, 'change' is understood to mean the managing of transitions.)

Discoveries within Theory U

- Change starts with 'a shift in the inner place from which we operate'. Scharmer calls this 'the blind spot of innovation'. It was always presumed that the starting point for change lies in actions that affect the outside world, by doing something you haven't done before. But Scharmer found that the real starting point lies with inner change. (This immediately has far-reaching consequences. We see that what happens in our body plays an important role in innovation processes and, along with the spirit-mind, the body is now an important component.) Scharmer says, "*Body and Mind are not one, and also not two*". To get in touch with what he means, you might want to try a little exercise, alone or in a small group. Ten years ago, Scharmer started a lecture, at the (then) PTT-telecom (where I worked at that time), with this exercise. After the exercise the atmosphere in this meeting had completely changed. The exercise is to think of the best piece of communication you ever made. Go back again, if possible, to your inner state at that moment. Once you are back in that inner place, describe this inner place to the others in the group (or to yourself) – this place from which you communicated so well. While writing this book I am also in a discussion with Otto about whether it really is about an inner space from where we act. If consciousness is around us, rather than inside us, than maybe we act from a place outside our body.

- *Working from the field*
That brings us immediately to his second brilliant finding: listening and acting from the field. It is a form of perception that shifts from active and focussed listening to hearing what the field wants to tell you. This is perceiving with all your senses: your body, heart, soul and mind. It is even possible to do this in a group, where the group becomes a 'social body' and perceives (almost) as one. When this happens it is impossible for any individual in the group to 'own' the insights and perceptions. Ego needs to be suspended, albeit temporarily. Acting from the field can be done just as effectively alone as it can in a group. You experience it more as 'being acted', rather than acting from the will or in expression of an idea. In a group this results in what is called co-creation: when ideas arise that none of the individual participants could have thought of alone. Scharmer, Senge and colleagues call this inner state presencing, a combination of presence and sensing. It is from exactly this inner state that the germs of innovation or new perspectives arise. Or perhaps it is better to say, "*it is the state in which the germs of something new, something already existing in the field, can find us…*"
Constellations are one of the fastest ways I know to get into the state of presencing. But this is highly dependent upon the inner attitude of the facilitator and the degree to which he or she can support the participants to form a field.

- *The emerging future*
Why should we want to learn from the future rather than from the past? Learning from the past has the tendency to cause those pat-

terns to repeat that are precisely the ones we want to stop or change. But 'learning from the future, as it comes towards us' might offer the possibility to make inner shifts which allow old patterns to stay in the past and new patterns to emerge. This emerging future is totally different to 'our future' or 'the future I want for my company'. 'My future' is a movement from me towards the future. The emerging future is a movement that comes towards me whether I like it or not. If you are serious about the concept of the emerging future, then, suddenly, you are connected with a deeply philosophical way of being in the world. A place where, immediately, serious questions arise about the viability of society. The emerging future confronts you directly with the imperative of letting go, releasing into the now. Where does 'my' future, the one that I always dreamed of, meet the emerging future?

At this point I'd like to add something to Theory U that comes out of my systemic work. I have already discussed this, extensively, with Arawana Hayashi, a colleague of Otto Scharmer and also with Otto, although only superficially with him. However, the following resonated with them both.

For many people, change begins with the idea that the world is not okay as it is.

- From a systemic perspective, change begins when we take the world as it is. I consider this to be also the most essential thing I have learned from Bert Hellinger. It sounds much easier than it is. It means that war belongs to the world and, as a child of the sixties, I did not find it easy to truly accept this idea. Taking the world as it is, means agreeing with the fact that things went the way they went. Taking the world as it is, means agreeing that this is the only possible world in the here and now and that I am a product of this world. So I must stand in the last and most humble place in the order and act from there, in contact with reality as it now is and the future as it comes towards me. If you do not take the world as it is, then you place yourself above the world. Your are operating from a different inner place. There is another advantage in taking the world as it is: it becomes easier to see all kinds of social mechanisms and to discover how social systems work. Your perception becomes clearer. I think that 'taking the world as it is' and 'taking reality as it is' can give an enormous depth to presencing.

The U process

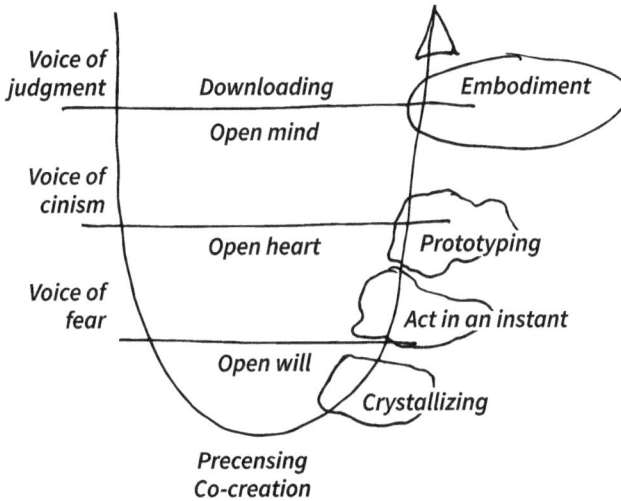

```
Voice of
judgment          Downloading              Embodiment

                   Open mind

Voice of
cinism

                   Open heart          Prototyping

Voice of
fear                                 Act in an instant

                   Open will

                                  Crystallizing

                   Precensing
                   Co-creation
```

Stages and phases in the U process

Theory U and all its stages are explicitly described in the book Theory U. What follows is a summary of the essence of the process and some remarks and additions from a systemic phenomenological perspective.

Four stages of listening, perceiving or assimilating information

The stages of Theory U complemented by knowledge from the systemic phenomenological perspective.

The first stage: Downloading

Downloading is the state in which I accept only precisely that information which confirms my view of reality. Once, when working in Brazil, a woman asked me how constellations differ from psychodrama. Intuitively, I didn't really know what to answer, so I asked her if she could see any differences. *"No"* she said. Later I heard that she was a psychodrama teacher. Apparently she was downloading; something in me recognised this and made me hesitate. If I had tried identifying all manner of differences between constellations and psychodrama what would have been the effect? Would she have been able to 'hear' me? Or would we have polarised into a debate, trying to convince each other and going ever deeper into our own states of downloading. Many change-managers do not like or want people, departments or organisations that are in the state of downloading. But resisting downloading only pushes people deeper into that state. Actually what is downloading, if seen systemically? It is being loyal to one's own system. Loyal to one's own world-view. These loyalties are accompanied by an enormous amount of passion! If you want to get access to people who are in a state of downloading, then acknowledge their passion and wonder to whom or what they are loyal. Just check for yourself to whom or to what are you being loyal when you are downloading and, crucially perhaps, what is required from you to get out of this state.

Voice of Judgement

It is inevitable that with downloading comes judgements. Judgements about other ideas, other ways of thinking, other life styles, other organisations, other systems. Judgements about almost everything. Systemically, though, judgements are rather interesting. What is a judgement trying to do? It is trying to protect something that is important to you and to set boundaries around that. But is it always trying to protect what is important to you personally? No. Quite often our judgements are trying to protect our family, our education, faith, religion, country of origin or organisation. The passion in the judgement goes beyond personal interest: it is loyalty to a larger group. You can check this by asking yourself this question: *"For whom or for what do I work so hard by having this judgement? What groups in society or what concepts or values am I trying to protect by having this judgement?"*

So if you want to move beyond the state of downloading, it is better to welcome judgements. And to take people as they are and to welcome them just as they are.

Many approaches to change and development, including presencing, are based on looking at the world without judgement. But, perhaps, in this state of being 'without judgement', lies a judgement about having judgements. So how can we know if being judgemental is better or worse than being non-judgemental? We know that judgements can lead to conflict and war, but how can we know if that is better or worse? Better or worse for whom? Maybe you find peace and harmony nicer than conflict and war, but maybe peace suits you as an individual, more than war does. How do we, and can we, really know what is better or worse? Perhaps our only choice is to try to enter a state beyond judgement, rather than to stop judging. If I am beyond judgements that means, for one thing, that I do not need to renounce my judgments – I have moved, perhaps only temporarily, beyond them. Accepting myself exactly as I am, makes it much easier for me to be open to something new.

The second stage: Open Mind

Open mind is the state in which it is all right for me if my worldview changes based on the information I receive. Maybe things are, after all, different than I have always imagined. It is also, perhaps, not so easy to admit that this new perspective might be true and meaningful.

I am still fascinated by how Al Gore's film An Inconvenient Truth gave people a new perspective on global warming. In the film, which is more PowerPoint show than film and presents information we have had for years, something happens that seems to open audiences up to another worldview than they brought with them to the cinema.

And there lies the key question: what helps people make the transition from downloading to open mind?

Voice of Cynicism

Before we move to Open Heart, the next stage in the U process, we need to address the cynic inside us. What is the purpose of the voice of cynicism? It tries to protect us! So, what does it protect? It protects the heart – by keeping it closed. Why would you not want to open your heart? To avoid feeling the pain again. The pain of a previous experience, when suddenly everything changed and you could not protect yourself. Lack of trust is a mild form of cynicism.

In a workshop by Arawana Hayashi, The art of making a true move, there was an Australian woman who had been unable to work for ten years but was about to re-enter the world of work and labour. She seemed to be a competent person but she said that sometimes she closed her heart and was cynical about the world. She was part of a small group doing the social-presencing activity of the U process, and her question was the focus of the group work. She said that she had lost her father as a ten-year-old girl when he stepped on a land mine in Korea while on army patrol. A very understandable reason for closing your heart, even if she was hardly aware of the connection between her cynicism and the loss of her father. A freeing, very emotional sentence, that arose from within the group was "From the position of the father, looking at his daughter, it is now permitted for you to survive when you step into a new or unknown field…"

Here it also might be useful to explore cynicism in the context of or-ganisational change. Such an exploration can uncover traumatic events from earlier in the organisation's or personal histories, thereby making it possible to heal the traumas.

The third stage: Open Heart

Open heart is the state of empathetic listening. Listening from the place of the other. And here something special happens, compared to the first two states of perception. With downloading and open mind we have to work with an 'I' and a 'you', a transmitter and a receiver. Separate systems, each with clear borders. With open heart the border between I and you becomes less distinct as these two (or more) systems begin to merge. This gives more possibilities for resonance between the two people and of course it also makes both a bit more vulnerable. It means opening your heart to the other one. Listening from the heart also means tapping into the intelligence of the heart. Using this source of wisdom about what works and what doesn't work. The source that knows what makes the heart start flowing. Projects that give the heart reason to flow have more chance to get that flow 'working' for them. If people can open their hearts to a project, they develop more confidence in the project.

Voice of Fear

Now, on the way to the next stage we encounter the Voice of Fear. Fear? Of what? Fear of letting go of what we know, that with which we are familiar. Fear of putting the ego and the will aside. Fear of not knowing where the next step will take us, and whether there will be firm ground under our feet. Not knowing whether we will fall or fly. So it is almost an irrational fear. Perhaps, if we were to look at the fear rationally, it would not be so terrifying.

The fourth stage: Open Will

This is the state of 'listening from the field'. If I fully expose myself to society, to this town or this organisation, what is it trying to tell me? Also known as presencing, this is the state of connecting with the source of all that is possible. It is totally in the here and now, still in contact with what was and also with the emerging future. When Otto Scharmer is in this state, and asks questions in a small group focussed around a particular issue, his questions have a different effect than if I were to ask exactly the same questions but from another inner state. This is also the state of co-creation, in contact with the possibilities that are already present in the field. Here the inner shift takes place, suddenly observing the world from another perspective. Getting stuck becomes an energy generator and burdens become blessings.

Travelling up the U

We have arrived at the bottom of the U, and are in the state of presencing: an inner attitude full of possibilities.

But how do we move on and up?

Crystallising

The state of crystallising arises after we release the old patterns. Crystallising is the state in which new patterns or ideas can emerge, like a new crystal that suddenly forms in a fluid full of ideas. This is not an active progress you can direct, neither is it about constructing new ideas, forms or projects, or re-implanting old wishes or dreams into the vacuum of an open soul. It is a passive but very focussed process. Something in the field crystallises.

It is the process of 'letting (something) come up', of "*Hey! This feels like it could be a great idea. Where did it come from!*" Systemic work has taught us that, following a constellation, the incubation time for this process can be from weeks to months and cannot be accelerated or forced. Just as a plant does not grow faster when you look at it all the time, or push some soil away to see if little roots have started to appear, a certain degree of patient waiting is needed for new crystals to form.

In constellations about social issues, for example in the question concerning the relationship between patient, nurse and budget in homecare, we saw that a constellation that clearly shows the impotence of the present situation is often needed first. (Admitting this impotence is a quick way to enter presencing.) Then we can do a second constellation, with the intention of letting come. In this spirit we might begin with a question such as "If we follow the movements in the field, and trust them, how might the relationship between patient, nurse and budget look?" And, delicately, like the forming of a new crystal, a possible new pattern appears. In this case, in the new pattern, the distance between nurse and patient became precise and held, in some way, the dignity and uniqueness of the patient as a human being. It appeared important, also, that the patient could see the budget and that it 'stood' close to the patient. All the participants in this co-creation constellation

---

*– managers, caretakers, advisors, patients and their families – felt that
a new pattern had emerged around which the organisation could crystallise.*

Arawana Hayashi introduced the Japanese concept of Ma – the state of
meaningful emptiness – into the U process. Ma is a form of stillness that
supports the crystallisation process. Ma goes a long way to creating the
conditions under which a new pattern or a new movement can find its way
to you. From out of the field of possibilities into you. Arawana's workshops
are marked by beautiful exercises, such as where a pair dances a duet that
arises and is led by the field. The first person enters the Ma state and waits
to be found by a movement. When this 'piece' is finished, the second person waits in Ma until a movement finds him or her. Then the first person
waits again in Ma until a movement finds her. After a while the movements
and the dancers begin to arise and flow together and forms appear that
neither of the two dancers knew or could have conceived alone.

Acting in an instant

Acting in an instant is more being acted than acting. It is more 'Something has been decided' than 'We have decided something'. Acting in an instant is acting without having considered the budget, the dangers, or even
whether its doable. It is acting from the source, acting from a changed
field, acting from a different inner place. It is acting that has no connection to old patterns.

This acting might achieve its destiny but it might also be doomed to
failure.

It's better to fail early instead of muddling through, for far too long, on
a hopeless path.

What often happens to me is that I look back, a few months after a constellation, and then suddenly see precisely the moment when I did act in
an instant.

What changes? The field or the structure?

As we move up the right-hand side of the U we come to Prototyping: the
stage of trying out on a small scale, followed by the stage of Embodying, in

which well-functioning prototypes can further evolve or be implemented in the larger organisation. As we go up the right side of the U, a lot of expertise still needs to be gained about how these processes occur. What is crucial here is to stay connected with the source accessed through the state of presencing, while entering the stage of prototyping and implementing.

I want to look more closely at the right side of the U, from the systemic view of the organisation as either field or structure.

What is it that actually changes, if something does change after a constellation or a presencing session? We investigated this by experimenting in an organisation with the help of one of its project leaders, a man called Henk, who was the issue holder in a constellation that delivered many new insights and perspectives about 'this' project.

After the constellation, when Henk had made some decisions and then introduced them to the project team, very little happened that was useful. There was resistance, there was discussion, but there was no new energy or flow.

In a second experiment, after a second constellation, Henk went to a contemplation room, a Ma room, where he had nothing specific to do. When he returned, something seemed to have changed. Not only in Henk, but also in the field around him: his energy had changed, he emanated something different. When Henk returned to the project group with his new energy, immersed in this new field, he didn't do or say much, he was simply different. But different in a way that had a far greater effect on the project group than the first time he tried to tell them about his decisions.

When you announce new decisions then you create a kind of structure. In the second experiment it really seemed that Henk carried a changed field into the project group. And that begs the question: *"What happens if a changed field meets a field that hasn't changed or has been changed in such a way that it is now travelling in a different direction?"* *"Which field seems to be the stronger?"* *"How can you create the conditions to make this a fruitful encounter?"* Presumably not by preferring the new field over the original field.

What we discovered is that Henk, although he had been deeply in the state of Ma and had a changed field around him, still encountered the Voice of Fear on his way from the contemplation room back to the project group. The quality of his fear had this character: "Something in or around me has changed. I cannot even give it a name or say what it is. It is taking me along with it. Now I am on my way to meet the project group again. I feel their loyalty to the old and familiar, and their ambivalence to me and the new that I bring. The new that carries possible disloyalty towards them. And I have no idea how or if this will work out. I have to abandon predicting the result of this encounter... maybe I have to rely on mechanisms I do not yet know well: perhaps those of resonance and consonance."

Resonance needs a transmitter and a receiver: one field sets the other in vibration. You listen to a musical performance and your heart starts vibrating 'in concert'. With consonance you can no longer distinguish a transmitter and receiver. The elements set each other in vibration and attune to each other in a creative process through which something new often arises. A pianist attunes to the hearts of the audience and the energy in the room and starts playing music that nobody, including the pianist, has heard before.

What we can be certain of, from our explorations, is that when the fields of Systemic Phenomenological Work and Theory U meet and unite, new and valuable knowledge emerges.

Part Three

Organisational themes from a systemic perspective During my time in this work, I have encountered many organisational themes that occur frequently. We'll now discuss seventeen of those themes.

Some of these themes came across my path as issues in one or more constellations. Often I was asked to expand on a theme from my own experiences and also, while writing this book, I made substantial notes about many more issues that merit further exploration. But we have enough: my goal is not to write exhaustively about every current organisational issue, but to give you a feeling for the systemic perspective.

Perhaps you will recognise certain situations that, wholly or in part, are directly applicable to your work or organisation. I wish that this book in general, and the following section in particular, help you to take action and make decisions that are beneficial, productive and clear.

III.1 Success

"*Success has the face of the mother*". This statement from Bert Hellinger, bizarre on first hearing, has kept me busy for a long time. Such a strange sentence! Yet, from the beginning, I felt a power in it.

Success starts with the 'taking' of life. Life comes through the mother. We do not own life nor does life own us: life flows into us and through us in order to create something in the world around us.

In this sense, success is a form of life energy flowing towards its destiny. When this flow is interrupted, the energy stagnates and 'pain' results. Sometimes the pain manifests as a headache; sometimes as indecision or bankruptcy.

Life energy that is flowing towards its destiny attracts others: investors, colleagues, clients. It creates a pleasant atmosphere. Try comparing, for example, shops, companies or schools that you know. Where is the life energy flowing more and where less? Where is it clearly present and where is its absence disguised by forced smiles or customer-focussed sentences lacking any sincerity?

It is a pleasure to meet professionals who are in contact with life energy. They display a passion for their profession and are open to the outside world.

By the way, success does not always mean more, more, more and bigger, bigger, bigger. Sometimes it means less. Sometimes it can be feeling more genuine, sometimes following your destiny (whatever that may be), perhaps leaving the organisation you liked and cared about so much.

Success acknowledges all the pivotal events from an organisation's past: the mergers, bankruptcy perhaps, the illnesses and the burned-out workers, the redundancies in times of downsizing, industrial accidents and so on.

Without these events, and their cost to the company and to society, the organisation would not be what it is now.

Success also acknowledges the future as it presents itself. This emerging future is bigger than the company's future and has another direction. The future of a company appears to go forward. The emerging future is the future of the world, of society as it comes towards us. Whatever it might be; whether we like it or not.

Success is in the now, in the flow of life as it flows through us.

What prevents success?

Is success allowed? To whom or what do you feel disloyal when success finds you?

Success strongly affects conscience. *"Do I still belong, now that I am successful?"* Success often requires taking a risk by crossing over the borders of our conscience.

Sometimes it is also difficult to face our own grandeur. In his or her modesty each human being is grand; each human being is a miracle. If we can really open up to our own grandeur, it unfolds to its full extent. This can be very difficult to see and to take. To accept life is sometimes more painful than to accept death.

There are many prejudices about success. One is the master and slave concept: the idea that if one person is successful, it must be at another person's cost. Prejudices are excellent for revealing hidden patterns. Patterns which entangle us and bring things to a halt.

Success is a primary emotion; a direct reaction to the world just as it is.

Success is not pursuing dreams or illusions. This tends to bring a kind of hollow or empty success often accompanied by excessive ego. Dreams or illusions are secondary emotions, arising from contact with inner images that want to change the past.

> " *Success starts when we take the world exactly as it is* "

Success is also modest. That is why this chapter is short and simple. Success is, by definition, always over, finished, done. Whoever lingers in success stays in contact with the past, with that which is over and done. Lingering in success is a good way of losing one's connection to the future.

Loss makes success complete. How? By acknowledging it, by facing it and by letting it pass. Letting go of loss opens up space and freedom for what follows, what wants to emerge. If we set free our loss, then the loss will set us free.

> " *Gratitude is a bigger source of happiness than plans for the future* "

Bert Hellinger

III.2 Business Transfer

"We've been closed since yesterday and I have an appointment with the solicitor, next Friday at 11 am, to sign the contract. But there is still so much to do: final repairs, paying the last bills and we haven't even started the stock inventory or begun clearing up."

This was a hectic-sounding Lisbeth, coming, thankfully, to the end of the transfer of her and her husband's small business.

It is in a small French town, a computer business with a shop which they started from scratch and built up over ten years. Her husband began it with initial financing from a cousin and soon Lisbeth became involved, with their son helping out from time to time. A typical family enterprise.

They had one employee – who was often ill – which made the long days even longer. But they attracted a band of loyal customers, supplemented by tourists dropping in to use the internet. As retirement age beckoned, the wish grew to have more time for themselves and to finish restoring the house they'd bought three years earlier. In the end, selling the business took over a year. Buyers came and went leaving only disappointment behind. It was more than a year before the first serious buyer came into the picture. But dared they hope that the sale would actually go through? That the bureaucratic banks might move just a little faster. Everybody is willing and working hard but the waiting is exhausting. As the months tick by everyone gets more nervous and restless, till the announcement comes that brings release...

How does a business transfer look, when viewed from a systemic perspective?

The seller

How do you really leave such a company? The company you founded, to which you gave the best years of your life and that became almost a part of you. Maybe you are unconsciously identified with the company. To your customers, you are the company and the company is you. Maybe the company has fulfilled something for you that could not be fulfilled in any other way?

This was the case with the owner of a sauna company which had become her 'baby'. The company had fulfilled her wish for a child, a wish that could not be fulfilled biologically. Selling such a business to a new owner takes very delicate handling: to whom do you entrust your child? How do you stop yourself from interfering with 'your child's' further development? Particularly if you are unhappy with the direction the new owner takes.

It is worth taking some time to consider what was solved for you by establishing your business. What wanted to be fulfilled? Was it an escape from unbearable pressures somewhere else in the system?

Take a systemic look at your company. Is it really 'your' company or did someone else in the family want to start a business but couldn't and, unconsciously, you did it for them? If so, then there is a founder behind the founder and it will help to honour them. Perhaps by commemorating them in the company history or with a plaque or a statue or naming the boardroom after them.

It is always a good idea to tell the new owner the full history of the company. How it was born and grew; all the ups and downs it experienced. From where and whom did you receive financial or moral support? Which customers stayed loyal and never let you down? Which customers are you glad never to have to deal with again? As you relate your story you will come to see that your company was probably much bigger than you thought. By mentioning all those systemic actors out loud, they become recognised again by you and also by the new owner. This should ensure that they will not trouble the new owner with old grievances. This 'storytelling' process really helps the seller to unpeel his or herself, bit by bit, from the business.

What about the family? Not only those who worked in the company, but all those who, in some way, felt a part of it. I've noticed that, quite often, brothers or sisters of the entrepreneur come to a constellations workshop with a question about the company of a family member. Even if they are not related in any official way to the company. Systemically, organisational relationships extend beyond just the business. Usually there are many more stakeholders than at first thought. Perhaps these stakeholders, too, should also be recognised in one way or another in the process of a business transfer.

Ownership

Perhaps you are legally and financially the owner. But are you also systemically the owner? You can found a company but does that automatically make you the owner? You cannot own life: life comes through you. You cannot own a child: you accompany and try to guide a child in their life for a while. If you want the company to do well for the new owner, how should you relate to it after the transfer?

First of all by cherishing all that it has given you in your life. By taking what was good and recognising every 'gift'.

Then by leaving behind all that you contributed and gave during the years it was in your care: your energy, your wisdom, the material and immaterial things. You do this with an inner statement like, for example, *"All the good I gave, you may keep. I did it with pleasure".* That is what you say to the company, first. Later you can do a similar ritual with the new owner.

And you should continue to look fondly at the company, while you get on with the rest of your (working) life.

You could see this process as a form of division of property whereby each system regains what belongs to it. So the systems of the organisation and the employee are disentangled, opening them both to new possibilities. As a new employee or new owner it is possible to notice, when you arrive for a function, take on a new job, or when you take over a company, whether or not a good division of property has taken place: the atmosphere of your predecessor is always still tangible in your new work environment. Sometimes this can be supportive, sometimes obstructive, sometimes even destructive.

Oh, and one more thing. If you, as the seller, gave your heart to the company, don't forget to take it back. This is the part you need for the rest of your life. I even know of a passionate businessman who, three times, gave his heart to the same company. Three times the company went bankrupt in his care. A few weeks after the third time he died of a heart attack. His wife said: *"This fits. He forgot to take his heart back…".*

Family businesses

When a family business is passed on to the next generation, a key question is to what degree the 'leaving' generation really can step back. This does not mean that the parents are no longer welcome in the company, but it does mean that the company is to be given, literally, into the hands of a son or a daughter. It needs to be done publically, with witnesses. It doesn't need to be 'official': a little party does just fine. The system needs this clarity and without it the clients are never really sure who is in charge; this dilutes their confidence in the company and the new owners.

An important question is also how 'clean' is the business that you hand over. Clean it 'systemically' before the transfer. Are there patterns from the past still wandering around the business? Patterns that might repeat if they are not brought into awareness?

The 56 year-old owner of a building company, already the seventh generation, comes to mind. He was the fourth son and, at a particular moment, he seized control of the business. Although his prompt and sudden action saved the company, it created a pattern of tension among the siblings because the natural order in the family system had been broken. This pattern had the tendency to repeat with the males of the following generation.

What could he have done to prevent this pattern repeating?

The three older brothers, who were bypassed by their younger brother (the current owner), could ease the tension, their younger nephews feel, by explaining that this tension belongs to their fathers' generation and not to them. Or the sons could be helped to understand that it is not within their power to rectify the situation for their fathers and uncles. (By giving everyone their rightful place in the system). That they do not have the 'task' or 'burden' to continue the pattern that exists between their fathers and uncles.

In this particular company something else, something very significant, had occurred: an uncle of the present owner had been shot during WW2. From the moment the uncle died, the war became a part of the company: every Remembrance Day was attended. The owner suddenly realised that the war had indelibly marked his company. When he became aware of this, he noticed that he did not want to pass this burden on to his sons. He wanted to deliver the company 'clean'.

The buyer

What is important for the buyer?

First, to find out how systemically 'clean' the company is. (This issue is covered in the previous section). It is also good to check if all the systemic debts have been paid:

- Is there anyone, perhaps clients, who paid a high price for the company's current success?

- From where or whom did the company get its initial investment? Were the funds 'contaminated' in any way?

- What about the premises? Was someone forced to move out so that these premises could be built?

- Has the company ever been bankrupt?

- Have there been workplace accidents that are still, in one way or another, in the collective conscience of the employees or the environment? Does the company feel like a safe place to work?

- What is the state of the energy and life force of the workers? If it is weak, is this a systemic solution, for an issue within the company, or does it belong to the employees themselves?

- Where did the name come from? The name is public property. Is it a name to continue with? How would the systemic owners, which includes the clients, respond or be affected if the name changed without their 'permission'? How often has the name changed in the past? How often has the logo been changed?

- Were there important grants or investors? Even if the debt has been paid financially, keep in mind that when one accepts a grant or gift, it also carries the ideas of the donor. Are those ideas still working in the business? Do they help or hinder?

- What are the guiding principles of the business you might purchase? Are these guiding principles compatible with yours?

- What do you actually want to buy? The building? The clients? The business's niche in society? The life force of the company? The business concept? The guiding principles?

- Are you ready to face everything about this company and the sale process? All the good and all the bad, both past and present. Be especially careful of those things to which you'd rather turn a blind eye...these are precisely the issues that will confront you if you become the owner.

- If you do buy it, what is it, in or for you, that the company will make whole or complete and vice versa?

- You are unlikely to be thinking about this now, but will the company continue after you leave (or sell it on) or will it end with you? For the company and, of course, for the employees this is important information. If the company will end when you leave, the employees must place their trust in the unknown. Trusting that, in some way, they will continue to be employed.

- Sometimes many things have to be changed in a company. Be clear if you are actually going to change the company or if what you intend, seen systemically, is to end this company and set up a new one.

This is a long checklist for a buyer who already has a thousand things to organise… but, whether you like it or not, the systemic conscience isn't interested in how busy you are.

> **"** *You cannot buy a company without also buying the fate of the company.* **"**
>
> *Jan Jacob Stam*

The transfer

Up till now we've been addressing the buyer, because everything we've discussed so far needs to be considered before the purchase takes place. But this raises an important question. Exactly when do you change from buyer to owner? When you sign the contract? Possibly. Or is it when the previous owner lets go of the reins and puts them directly into your hands? Clearly, there is a moment when the company belongs to no one. The present owner lets go and, for just a moment, there is nothing, a vacuum. Then you take the company into your hands. In that unseen, invisible moment is held the potential, the future of the 'new' company.

Of course there are many rituals that could be done by the seller and buyer. A party to mark the end and beginning. Something that includes the customers. Perhaps a small gift for the customers, shortly after the transfer, to remind them of how it was and to give a taste of how it will be. A gift that includes the freedom for the customer to choose again. Only the previous owner can tell the customers of his confidence in the new owner. He can do so quite precisely. Only authenticity will contribute to a successful business transfer.

III.3 Fraud

Whenever a person commits fraud they are fired immediately. Apparently, they had crossed the boundaries of the social group-conscience to the extent that they lost the right to belong to the organisation. Is it preferable, then, as usual, to cover up the fraud as soon as possible, to make it invisible to both the organisation and the world outside?

So... are we finished with the subject of fraud or dare we to venture further, into the systemic background of fraud?

And if we dare, how can we begin to look deeper into 'systemic' fraud?

We do so by asking ourselves, "*For what could fraud be a solution?*" This type of uncomfortable question implies that something more is at stake, that it isn't simply a dishonest act by someone. Another question quickly follows-on from the first, "*What has this act of fraud settled, put into a more healthy relationship? What balance, in giving and taking, did this fraud repair?*"

These questions invite you to consider the background of the perpetrator, but also the background of the organisation or society where the fraud took place.

When the cause originates with the perpetrator

The first check is to see if the perpetrator was wronged, personally, in their life, or if someone or something fell seriously short of the perpetrator's expectations. In this situation, it's clear for what the fraudster is seeking compensation.

But fraud can also be motivated by an unconscious pattern. Then it is worth identifying if someone was disadvantaged seriously in earlier generations; perhaps even a whole family. If we could hear the (fraudster's) unconscious, it might say, "*I am putting things right on your behalf, dear xxxx*". Then the question to the perpetrator is, "*For whom, in reality, did you commit this crime?*"

When the cause originates with the organisation

If fraudulent practices occur in a particular organisation more than one might expect, then you might ask yourself if this organisation has ever been involved in, or guilty of, creating a serious imbalance in giving and taking.

For example, when we see the wealth of the canal houses in Amsterdam, we might wonder who paid a high price for this wealth to be accumulated? Is it strange then, when Dutch development aid to so-called 'underdeveloped' countries, cannot be repaid by the countries who receive this money?

In organisations where fraud is frequent, a kind of unconscious co-creation can be taking place between perpetrators and the 'victim' organisation.

A senior civil servant from the Mexican ministry of health was quite moved by what she saw when she brought her issue into a constellations workshop: there was so much fraud and so much money never got to the people for whom it was meant: to the sick. To my surprise the audience began whispering and sniggering. Without thinking, I put this question, more to the audience than to the civil servant: "Do you think there exists the intention to put an end to this fraud and cheating?" Then the audience became totally silent. Immediately it became clear that we were involved with a much larger social theme. It is very possible that the theme of chronic fraud and malpractice is rooted in the socio-cultural history of that country, and yet it could still be a perpetrator-victim dynamic.

This leads us to a completely different aspect of fraud, quite removed from the simple concept of cause and effect.

What is the effect of fraud on the rest of the system? In every case involving fraud, that I have seen, this was a significant problem. In the Mexican example, the civil servants no longer dared to look their colleagues directly in the eyes. As if a blanket of shame lay over the whole system, bringing symptoms similar to those of trauma: the flow disappears and contact among co-workers becomes broken; they lose connection with each other and with the guiding principles of the organisation.

I clearly remember working with a Director of Social Services. Like the Mexican civil servant, he was also very saddened by the fraud in his organisation. At one point he said, almost desperately, to his colleagues, "This doesn't involve you. It is about one particular person". His colleagues responded with "That's nonsense; we are all involved!"

This was an important insight. That it does not help the system when the crime is investigated and justice is done (although this must take place). It is a misunderstanding to think that by isolating the event the workers will become comfortable and productive again. To isolate the incident and conceal the fraud is a recipe for prolonging the agitation in the organisation and repeating the pattern in the future. Here, again, what really heals is facing the reality of what is and realising that whatever caused the fraud to be committed continues to affect the whole system.

III.4 Justice

Through her tears, a woman says that her husband has begun a legal process against a large company. He had been providing services to it, but its new management cancelled his contract.

I tell the woman there is not much I can do for her, but that her husband is welcome to come if he wishes. The woman comes to see me during the break and thanks me because she feels recognised in her involvement.

In the intensity of the workshop I forget about our exchange, but the following morning her husband comes to the workshop. He is well dressed, probably in his early forties. He was supposed to be in Hanover that day but does not want to miss the opportunity he has been offered to enquire into his struggle. So he has postponed his appointment. Outside the room where we do the constellations, he confides to me that he has Parkinson's Disease and that the more emotional he becomes the more his hands start trembling. He agrees that I can share this with the participants.

His main wish is to know exactly what happened in the courtroom yesterday afternoon. When I ask him what is at stake in the legal case, he says it is about the compensation he believes is due to him.

As soon as he and the organisation stand opposite each other an enormous field of tension is felt: the kind of tension that narrows your perspective. Each party feels bigger than the other and this is also the only thing each can see: the subjective power balance in their relationship.

As soon as the lawyers of the two parties come in to the constellation, the field of tension shifts to the lawyers. For them it is clearly more about prestige than content and, again, the only thing that matters is how big each of the legal teams feels in relation to the other. It looks like a fight between two peacocks. The judge is not a part of the field of tension and none of the parties sees the judge or considers him to be of any importance;

During all of this, the client is very present, concerned and tense and has no doubt that what the constellation is showing is exactly what took place in the courtroom. He displays a very keen eye for detail, expressed in questions like "Exactly how does this lawyer feel towards that one?"

For the whole audience it becomes increasingly clear that this lawsuit will come to nothing. But the client is being drawn into it, as if by a whirlpool. Increasingly, the two parties see each other less and less.

In order to give a larger perspective I suggest adding an element for 'Whatever this is really about.' When this element is placed, everything changes. First of all the complainant (the husband) can finally say that his issue is really about recognition. Recognition of all that he has supplied to the company and of its quality. This also creates the first moment of contact – in the constellation – between the man and the company he has taken to court.

But even more important is that the complainant, the client, embraces the element "Whatever this is really about" and then they leave the field together. Later, it becomes clear that the real issue is the man's illness and how much time is left for him.

Justice does not exist

From the systemic perspective there is no such thing as justice. The more we strive for justice 'against' someone or something, the more we project onto the 'other' what we lack in ourselves. Striving for justice leads to escalation and war. Both parties become increasingly entangled in the web of their own personal conscience, their own ideas of good and bad. And if one of the parties is judged, in some way, to be right or wins the conflict in another way, there is a good chance that the pattern will repeat itself later. Either between the same parties or between others in the system.

What is the way out?

The solution is to move beyond the limits of the personal conscience around good and bad; this requires a lot of inner strength, discipline and fortitude. Sometimes it also requires detaching oneself from everyone who supports or encourages your fight for 'justice'. Those who support and encourage are also acting from their own personal conscience about right and wrong, and so they enforce the field of polarisation.

Going beyond the field of right and wrong carries the risk that you become disloyal to those who supported you, and that can be a high price to pay. Going beyond also means giving up any idea that you are better than the other party. Even when you do manage to rise above the field of right and wrong, and the other does not, you are still no better than them.

The client (the woman's husband) left confused but satisfied. He cancelled his appointment in Hanover.

" *Out beyond ideas of wrong doing and right doing, there is a field. I will meet you there.* **"**

Rumi

III.5 The glass ceiling

The glass ceiling is a term used for the invisible barrier that (many believe) prevents women from achieving higher functions in organisations and society. Usually this phenomenon is seen as resulting from deep-seated habits and ideas about the roles of women and men.

But there is also a systemic aspect to this phenomenon, seen especially with so-called father's daughters. These are women who find themselves standing next to their father, in the mother's place, or in between their father and mother. Not because they consciously want to, but because something in the relationship between their father and mother was or is missing. Perhaps love could not flow between the father and mother. Perhaps they simply could not be fully present in their relationship. Most often this inability to be completely together has its origins in events that happened in their own lives, like the death of a first love or the father or mother being systemically entangled in their own family of origin.

This causes, so to say, a hole in the system, at the layer of the parents, which sucks a child into it. If it is a girl, then she often becomes a father's daughter.

This is how the system solves the problem of the hole: it sucks someone else in to fill it, to take that place.

No blame can be attached to the one who is sucked in, to father's daughters (or, in different contexts, mother's sons). You can't blame dust for being sucked into a vacuum cleaner: the pull is just too strong. Systems, whether family or organisational, are very strong vacuum cleaners.

Family systems are an excellent breeding ground for patterns. Because, for most people, the family is the first system they encounter and also, as these patterns are formed at such a young age, we are mostly unaware that these patterns are forming.

Growing up in a systemic pattern has two main consequences:

1. Later in our lives, as we become members of other systems, such as work, sport or our own families, the patterns from our family of origin tend to reappear. For example, in your work a pattern that has its origin in your family of origin is triggered and repeats.

It is very rare for you to notice immediately that the pattern actually does not really belong to your work situation.

It is a common misunderstanding that, in this situation, we should work on our personal patterns first. This is neither necessary nor desirable if we wish to improve the workplace situation: it is sufficient to separate the patterns in the workplace system from the patterns originating in the family system.

2. The second consequence of growing up in a pattern (and all of us grow up in multiple patterns) is that we develop particular coping-strategies and skills, precisely tailored to that family system. As we grow to adulthood within these systems, we unconsciously develop many valuable qualities as we learn how to survive within the patterns which, outside of our awareness, are controlling aspects of our behaviour, and cause us sometimes to suffer. You can find a description of these common patterns in my book Fields of Connection.

What, typically, are the skills a father's daughter develops? At what does she excel? Father's daughters can be extremely sensitive, feeling exactly what someone, at a near or higher layer in the order, lacks or needs. Often even before the father, or the manager/director has noticed that they lack something. For the same reason most father's daughters are good at arranging and organising what is needed. Father's daughters are rarely impressed by authority; they know how authority works and can even play games with it. For this reason father's daughters are often career early achievers, rapidly climbing the employment ladder.

Father's daughters are often excellent sparring partners for directors. Someone with whom they can talk through the affairs of the company at the end of the afternoon. Not only about those issues that are common knowledge, but also what might be worrying the director or what he feels unsure about. Actually, the father's daughter often fulfils the function of the sparring partner the director cannot find within his management board.

A father's daughter can tell it like it is. Can tell the director the truth that others often don't dare to do, especially when the director has a very powerful position. Directors like to have someone they can trust to point out their blind spots. These exchanges make the system complete again.

Another important quality of father's daughters is that are good at bringing together what was separated, at repairing broken relationships, bringing people or factions together; mediating if necessary.

Other functions where father's daughters usually feel totally at home include policy functions, deputy directors, internal or external consultants and so on.

There is a price or two to pay, however, for the qualities gained by living through this pattern. In organisations, father's daughters are often sucked into higher hierarchic layers, creating jealousy among colleagues in the department: *"Who does she think she is?"*. The price of such success can be loneliness.

The other price to pay comes out of the fact that the original pattern can exist so long as it does not become public knowledge. A part of the mother secretly agrees to her daughter being sucked into the hole between her and her husband... as long as it is never spoken about. This pattern is taboo, it is forbidden.

And that is exactly the systemic aspect of the glass ceiling. When a father's daughter, after a successful career, suddenly is appointed to be the managing director or president of the board of directors, what can happen is that, deep inside, something says *"This feels strange, fulfilling this role so publicly. This is too exposed."* and *"Oops, there is no inner permission to take this role"*. Often, then, a kind of withdrawal takes place.

The solution? First, to become aware of this pattern.

Next to become aware of all the skills and qualities that were developed growing up in this pattern.

The next step is to realise that the organisational system is different from the family (of origin) system.

So, from where could the permission come to fully take the directorship role? Well, actually from the mother. Father will always support his daughter. Often father's daughters experience tension or conflict with their mother. Permission from the mother's side implies to accept the mother and everything that comes through the mother and her female line.

III.6 Taking leave and saying goodbye

Sabine, sitting next to me, has been hesitating for a long time. She tells me that in a month she will resign from her company to start a, as yet unknown, new professional life. She radiates ambivalence. I do not know whether I should congratulate her or commiserate with her. Maybe I feel what she feels. After all, it is tangible in the air around her. Her eyes dart back and forth and her face alternately radiates crying and laughing. She looks about thirty-five.

What she wants to do is to say goodbye, but she doesn't really know how to do that well. This has been her first important job and she has grown enormously in it. Now she feels it is time for new adventures, new challenges.

Sometimes growth just wants to grow. Even if you do not like it. It can happen that you ask someone about a next step. *"Have you already decided?"* And the answer is *"No"*. But if you then ask: *"Has 'it' taken its decision?"*, the answer is often: *"Yes"*. It seems that sometimes the field or your unconscious or your body has already decided for you. Neuro-physicists have established that someone can start acting even before neurons fire in the brain.

It also seems to be important to listen to the inner announcements of the next step. These are subtle signs, not sudden impulses to do something else. More like the way spring gently announces its arrival.

The suddenly deciding to do something else has an impulsive quality, often carrying a sense of 'the right time is just a bit later'.

The messages from deeper layers often arise slowly. But if they are there, listen to them. Spring comes but once each year... and next spring might be quite different.

Saying goodbye to colleagues

So it was with Sabine: she knew she had to go, to leave the organisation and her first job, even without knowing what was coming next.

We do a ritual with her. She chooses representatives for those who have been significant for her in one way or another.

She places someone to represent the manager who mentored her in the company and who apparently meant a lot to her. She stands opposite him and her eyes fill with tears. Obviously, he was more to her than just her boss. In a way he was also the father she never had, encouraging her to persevere and showing confidence in her abilities. So she actually has to say goodbye to two images. The image of the manager who helped her to find her place and also the image of the organisation as her substitute parental home. Sabine's awareness that both images had merged into the person of the manager reflects and honours the situation. Acknowledging this reality liberates both the system that remains and the person who leaves.

Next, Sabine chooses someone to represent a colleague. She stands opposite this woman, with a slightly tense attitude and holding her head a little bit higher than their actual difference in height. For Sabine it is liberating to acknowledge that she sometimes felt better than this colleague, that sometimes she turned her nose up at her. No regret, just acknowledging that it was as it was.

After some more of these mini-rituals Sabine feels that she is ready now. She feels, quite precisely, that this is enough.

Taking leave in a good way is at least as important in an organisation as making a good entrance. Good leave-taking is important for both parties, for the one that leaves but also for the one that remains. It ensures both parties are free and open for something new. When an individual leaves an organisation well, it also benefits the organisation by leaving that employee's function clean and free of systemic entanglements. Then it is easier for a successor to come in and flourish.

For the leaver, whatever the reasons for leaving, it is also good to be free and clean again. Otherwise you are less available for the labour market. A future employer feels this immediately you show up for the job interview.

If the departure was painful, then it can sometimes take a while before a person is really able to leave the system. But, just as with Milton Erickson's phrase: *"It is never too late to have had a happy childhood"*, it is also 'never too late to have a growth-sustaining cv'.

The question is, to what extent is it a good idea to accept a pay-off, in money or in work, when you leave a company. A half-hearted goodbye is a recipe for confusion and loss of energy and drive.

Taking leave from guiding principles

Thomas is a vicar. In his early forties, he is lively with a playful look in his eyes. Something in him has decided to leave the church. He does not want so much to leave the people or the organisation, but he wants to say goodbye to the guiding principals of the church, his church. Its guiding principles are:

- *Salvation is not for priests*

- *Suffering leads to happiness*

- *Then the guiding principle he does not even dare to say out loud, "because that would blow the system apart…" a future is not permitted.*

Later Thomas explains that, in his opinion, the last principle focusses the church on the past. In a long process Thomas once more opens himself to these three principles that have made him what he is now. His girlfriend sits at his side and sobs. With deep respect, like a monk in prayer, Thomas once more articulates these guiding principles. After a while he turns to face the rest of his professional life, his future.

When you have worked somewhere for a long time, it can be equally important to say goodbye to the guiding principles of the organisation, or department, where you worked. An organisation represents something and it is worthwhile to give due consideration to what extent you and it are interwoven. To know what you want to take with you and what you want to leave behind. This implies something larger than just taking leave from your colleagues and 'your' organisation. Some organisations also belong to a field. Some of these fields are strong and require strong forces to set in motion a change. In the Netherlands, for example, the fields of medicine and education are very powerful and hard to move or change. The church, almost everywhere in the world, is a powerful field. What does 'to take leave from a field' mean? What does it ask of a person?

I have always had a love-hate relationship with the consulting firm where I learned much of what I know about organisations. From most of the principles of that firm I took my leave, said farewell. But the founder of that company taught me something that, every day, I still value: *"Allow companies their misery"* he said. Maybe this was also the germ around which my systemic work in organisations grew. The founder of this consultancy firm no longer lives but I am still grateful to him for this, rather unusual, guiding principle.

III.7 Dismissal

Disguised dismissal

The human resources managers at a big hospital are a bit desperate. One of their responsibilities is conducting the internal job-flexibility policy. Among other things, this means they are given the task of finding a 'new' role for people who are no longer needed (or wanted) or who do not function well in their current department. Often this is really just disguised dismissal from one department and the hope that a job can be found again, in a different department. Such a dismissal is not really spoken out; absolutely not by the manager of the department. The HR advisors say: "Our job description states that we should tell the employees to leave, but it feels so strange to do this."

From a systemic perspective also it is strange. The HR adviser has actually assumed the manager's role. Saying *"No"* to someone is not easy; we all know that. It feels much nicer to say to someone he can stay than to say to someone he has to leave. But the only person who can tell someone they have to leave is their manager and it must be face to face, with eye contact. This is the only form of No that works and supports growth.

The organisation takes priority

The survival of the organisation prevails over retaining employees or job-functions. A people-oriented HR policy can appear to be at odds with this principle. But that is only how it looks. If you keep a function that is not necessary for the survival of the organisation, or you keep an employee because it is 'human' to do so, it is not a respectful act. Not for the function, not for the employee and not for the organisation.

Maintaining unnecessary functions undermines the organisation. In the end employees also feel and know this. But this is not an excuse for making the employees feel responsible for their own dismissal. When a manager who must dismiss one or more people appeals to his employees for sympathy, "*You can see for yourselves how the market has shrunk*" he or she loses strength. Crucially, though, the pain of the dismissal is diminished. Feeling this pain is necessary: it purifies those dismissed and, sometimes, also those who stay behind. Without the pain of purification it can be difficult to feel, once more, the force of growth.

To Brazil… where Eduardo buys a fruit drink company and invests a substantial amount in the enterprise. But the company seems stuck; it's not working any better than it did with the previous owners. The company is based in a town where, some ten years earlier, many companies went bankrupt due to the global financial crisis. The mayor of the town is socially-minded and is looking for investors to provide employment. So Eduardo bought the drink company and is doing everything possible to breathe new life into it. What is remarkable is that, just like many other business owners and directors, he and his family live out of town. As he describes the town, an image emerges of a ghosttown, a town of lost souls.

Unconsciously, Eduardo believes his investment will reinvigorate his employees. He thinks that if he gives enough, the employees will start giving too and systemic exchange and growth of turn-over will begin. But there is another principle at work. The loyalty of the employees – who kept their jobs – to their colleagues – who were dismissed – is bigger and stronger than the energy of the new investment.

Eduardo, becoming aware of this principle of loyalty, realises now that

---

he has one last chance: he must visit every family of a dismissed worker and listen to their stories. He knows he must give their pain a respectful place. This is a completely different investment to that which he thought was needed but, immediately and intuitively, he feels this is the way forward.

The line

How do you dismiss a person who 'crossed the line' in some way? Someone who did something that went so far over the boundaries of personal conscience, that he or she can no longer belong? You do so by simply and clearly saying how it is: *"You crossed the boundaries of what we stand for, of what is important to us".*

Why this way, these words? Because this gives priority to the organisation and prevents unwanted and counterproductive patterns appearing in the organisation. Perhaps, through this process, you do not only dismiss the person, but also the seed of an unwanted pattern. Such a dismissal should neither be blown up to 'We want to set an example' nor be swept under the carpet. Both are overreactions that ensure the pattern's absence is only temporary and encourage the pattern to surface again.

III.8 Entrepeneurship

I receive an e-mail from a person we'll call 'M', asking: *"… from a systemic perspective, what does a self-employed person need to create a successful business and position oneself in an already crowded market?*

How do I, being on my own, ensure the viability, the flow of my business? Who and what are part of it? What makes the system of an independent contractor flourish?"

My response was as follows:

Hi M,

This is a good question! A few years ago I didn't even know what ZZP [1] actually meant. Looking at it systemically this is a monster of a term. 'Without personnel' – as if you lack something! Suddenly the Netherlands has become overrun by ZZPs. Sometimes it seems like a proud nickname. The world of a ZZP is not always a bed of roses. I know the feeling myself. For a long time I saw myself as someone who would be 'in employment'. That is how it went in my family. Nobody was self-employed. Even when I was co-owner of a consultancy firm, it still felt like being employed. Then I made the big step to work for myself. Again such a bizarre term. If you work for yourself, how can you be in service of the world? Working for yourself will take you into a disaster scenario. Perhaps it means not working for a boss anymore. What is wrong with having a boss? The more you let it sink in, the more you can feel that working for yourself could lead to cutting yourself off from your roots and from the market. The market is not waiting for somebody who is working for herself, as such a person is likely to be too self-absorbed to be really available for the market.

So… how might we name this step in our professional development. With care certainly. 'A step into the unknown?' 'Becoming an independent entrepreneur?'… or am I nit-picking here?

Initially, when you start to work independently, just like immediately after a birth for example, there comes a kind of romantic euphoria. "*Freedom at last! Finally I can do what I want, what I like and what I am good at!*" But then you notice that there seem rather a lot of ZZPs in the world. Dauntingly more than you ever imagined. Many of them seem to be at least as creative as you, with even better websites and working in the same field. You start comparing… comparing yourself with others is the first energy loss. Then the blow of realising that you have to do your own prospecting, find your own customers and do your own accounts – even though you have hardly any clients. And you need a space where you can work in a pleasant way. And, and, and…

Ok, enough euphoria and depression, let's look at it from a systemic perspective.

---

[1] In Dutch: *Zelfstandige Zonder Personeel*. Literally translates as Independent Without Personnel.

What do you leave behind when you decide to become an independent entrepreneur? Maybe a job where you were employed and enjoyed safety, protection, continuity and the certainty that there was always work there waiting for you. Work and clients that came to you as a result of the efforts, skills and perseverance of others. A company name that you felt a part of. A guaranteed salary and your insurance and pension all arranged for you. Maybe it is good to feel gratitude for all that, perhaps, you took for granted at the time, but which was fought for by many people over many years. That was the platform from which you 'launched yourself'. It was the ground of your work and cultural roots.

You can immediately feel, when you're with someone who wants to become independent, if he or she has taken their previous job fully into their heart… or if they are dismissive of it, talking about it as if it was just something temporary or something not to be proud of.

Often, our first 'job' has to do with something that could not be completed in our family system. A grandchild studies for the same degree that grandmother could not begin because the war started. Yesterday, I had a coaching interview with a successful entrepreneur who had a bad relationship with his father, but knew that he had built the company his father would have wanted.

So when you take the step towards independent entrepreneurship, ask yourself this question: Who, in your family background, would support you, would start beaming if he or she saw you now? We are talking about independent entrepreneurship, but what does independent mean here? How do we, in the independent entrepreneurship, make our system complete? There lies a huge energy source. Bring in the founder behind the founder. Put her picture on the wall in your office. It will be almost the first thing your client will see and appreciate, when he comes to visit you.

What is entrepreneurship? For sure it means taking risks. Becoming unfaithful towards yourself. Crossing your own borders and facing the unknown. This gives you strength.

It also means saying *"No"*. Or in any case it means a good balance between yes and no. Too much yes to clients and you feel yourself weaken, too much no makes you unreliable. *"You should create shortage"*, my former tutor used to say. But what he meant was you should be able to say *"No"* when appropriate.

Before completing this part about your professional and family background, you might just wonder if there were or still are obstructive patterns in that background, waiting to surface in your company. For example, a previous bankruptcy, an industrial accident or an environmental disaster.

This is important for the flow of energy in your company. Energy will stream when we take life exactly as it is and pass it on exactly as it is. This is not like passing-on a relay baton. Life flows through you and wants to continue flowing. This allowing of an unrestricted flow is irresistible to your clients.

Quite an undertaking!

And M, what needs to be done in a one-person company? Actually, all the functions of a normal organisation. (Have a look again at the chart of functions in Chapter I.4: Organisations want intrinsic order).

Leading the functions are those of agency, which you use to determine the territory, the playing field of your activities, to make contact with your competitors and 'colleagues', to go to trade meetings and to stay abreast of market developments.

Then the core functions. What it is that you really are offering to (your) customers or contributing to society. Or rather where is your passion and what makes your heart beat a little faster. Is it coaching, physiotherapy, looking after the demented elderly, doing peoples' accounts, producing tents and so on.

"I'm really disappointed!" said a self-employed man, when he noticed how much administration activity was needed to run a company on your own. *"I am still too busy getting a shape and structure to my business to start looking for clients"*, was his next observation. Unfortunately, it is indeed an illusion that you only need to focus on your core qualities in order to run your own business.

Next comes the question of where marketing and acquisition belong. Should they come before the core functions or after them. Before means that your core qualities would be in service of marketing. You could then expect to have a more market-focussed approach. But then you will have to like it! And if you like it, you'll learn naturally.

I was really surprised to realise that I like so much to be in contact with the market. For example when I started a publishing company I loved to talk with the buyers in the bookshops about how they went about book purchasing.

If the marketing function comes after your core functions, then marketing is in service of your core functions. Your approach would be more of a professional, a specialist, someone at the top of their profession. Then your professionalism would be a key message of your marketing.

In a way this is also the profile of the Dutch Hellinger Institute: we want to be at the cutting edge professionally. That requires also a lot of development time and keeping up-to-date with developments around the world. And, sometimes, you find you've taken a cul-de-sac.

> **"** *Wisdom is knowing what works and what does not work.* **"**
>
> *Gunthard Weber*

I learned a lot from this insight and I find it especially applicable to entrepreneurship. It is really not so difficult to feel what works and what does not work in this world. This feeling rises above personal conscience. On the level of personal conscience the question is, *"Who or what do I want to please with my offer"*. Knowing what works and does not work also rises above the (unconscious) collective conscience of systemic entanglements. Knowing what works is an inner knowing, in resonance with a larger force, in resonance with your destiny, that which you have to do in the world and makes an impact in the world. Knowing what works also implies the art of not doing. 'Fail early' and take the consequences, instead of wasting your energy flogging a dead horse.

What about the support and administration functions. Who answers the phone? Who answers e-mails? Who maintains the website? Who makes the coffee? Who does the books and deals with the tax authorities and so on?

Perhaps the business needs more investment? Does the new investor become the owner, part-owner or a sleeping-partner? Perhaps a loan would be better? Is the loan interest free? Must it be repaid by a set date? Is there a nagging desire to pay it off as soon as possible?

A nice exercise is to put A4 sheets on the floor for all these functions, in a half moon crescent. Take your time to stand on each sheet and feel how much energy you get from each function and how much energy it takes just to stand there. Check in with yourself in your own business and see how much time you spend on each of the functions. If you wake up one morning, after a bad night when your business was keeping you awake, look at which function you were busy with? Where would you go for help?

Well M., we've made a good start: first what was behind you, then what you left behind you without disconnecting from it. Then we visited all the systemic functions in your business. Are we done yet?

Work and family

Who stands next to you? Your family? To what extent do they participate in your business? Have you unknowingly started a family business? How do you ensure that your family is and always will be a different system, without being cut off from it or being too symbiotic? Does your website biography say that you're a mother, or would you rather clients didn't know this? Whether you are the breadwinner for your family or not, is yours a fully-fledged business with its own force and dignity or, from the family's perspective, has it more of a secondary quality? Work or family, which system has priority?

Our business began at the kitchen table. We had only one telephone line for the whole house so, often, one of our children answered when a client called. For a year or so that was okay until we began to feel that we were asking too much of our children. It also made some of our clients uncomfortable. The systemic entanglement became especially clear when we took on a secretary whose desk was in the room beside the children's room. On the one hand this very loyal secretary liked working in a family and hearing the children's stories when they came home from school. On the other hand she felt like an intruder. What I am trying to say is that even if you do not have a secretary, you can still easily become an intruder in your own family system.

Working in several systems, though, always gives a certain special charm and force which clients really can feel.

I recall meeting the (then) business woman of the year, while we both were presenting to a group of nursing-home directors. She talked about how her weekends were sacred for her and also of how she needed a lot of sleep to cope with all the impressions of her day. She expressed this in such a way that you could feel how well she balanced her work and family systems without excluding either of them. I remember the directors, who were all males, scratching their heads when they realised they had cut their family systems off from their work systems. To me they clearly seemed drier, with less flow and juice than this woman. It was as if their masculinity, their being-a-lover or being-a-father was not allowed to flow when they functioned as a director. By talking about her family, without naming it explicitly, being-a-woman-and being-a-mother was a part of the hardworking life of this woman.

That was clearly good for the flow in her company.

Here it is all about the difference between distinguishing and excluding. The businesswoman made a clear distinction between her work and private life, without excluding either of the two fields. This allowed aspects of her private life to be expressed in her work and to contribute to the flow. The nursing-home directors had strongly separated their work from their families: being in their work excluded their family and vice-versa. Some would call this a 'professional distance'. Although this gave them a kind of natural protection, the personal qualities that made them good partners or fathers could not flow in their function as directors.

Viability

So, M., now you are asking about viability. Well, viability is supported by starting at an appropriate size. Neither bigger nor smaller than you are. It means being totally authentic; being satisfied with smaller profits in the beginning, especially since these are the fruits of your labours. This is the kind of profit that makes you shine and feeds your self-esteem. So true growth begins. And with it comes increased success and a growing pleasure in your work. More people know who you are and what you do and, increasingly, you stand fully in life with energy to spare. It is the kind of growth that you can reinvest in yourself. If you find something that really gives you energy, stay with it for a while. Become good at it. Word-of-mouth advertising is much more important than paid-for advertising or sales strategies. Glowing, happy customers will bring you all the business you need.

It's still necessary to ensure that the market can find you while you are busy finding the market. When I asked my teacher in Germany if there was a market for organisational constellations, he said: *"Yes. But you should create it yourself".*

That was good advice. If you are starting-up a business, assume that you have to make your own market.

What should you do when you lose touch with your passion?

Stop!
Do not go muddling along.

Stop, even if you do not know what will come in its place. Make a conscious choice to accept perhaps months of chaos, disappointment and not knowing. Until you are clean again and feel the clarity needed for your next step.

"Dear M.,

This was a long answer to your simple question. Good luck!
Warm regards,

Jan Jacob"

III.9 Stuck!

Most of us, at first, try to deny that we are stuck.

I did just this, last summer in the Alps, on a day when I had planned to go paragliding (a sport I adore), but found myself stuck in our hotel due to bad weather. But I convinced myself that blue skies were just around the corner.

Being stuck occurs frequently. Usually it starts with a just a little bit of friction but then the system begins to turn more and more stiffly. At first you make small adjustments but, insidiously, signals appear. You fly off the handle at someone; you feel reluctant or you feel a stone in your stomach. Then the messages begin to come thick and fast: in each film we see or in each book we read, there is a character who tries to tell our unconscious what is happening.

If you do not admit or recognise it, you'll find it is not very funny to be in that pre-stuck phase. It feels like failure. But here is the secret. There is a lot of energy in being stuck and also, really, a lot of fun!

Exercise we learned from Arawana Hayashi.

Feel where you are stuck at this particular moment. Is your stuckness a nice big-one or a small-one? Ask your friends or colleagues to help you. Not to solve your problem or even to give you advice.

You want them to help you to get even more stuck.

Tell them how it feels in your body, this being stuck. For example: "I try to delegate something but it stays with me as if it's glued to my hands". *Your friends help you, with their hands, to push back into your hands what you want to get rid of. And you give them directions:* "No matter how I shake my arms, I can't let it go. Shaking my arms is becoming increasingly difficult". *So your friends hold your arms so that shaking them feels more and more terrible. And when it all feels too heavy, a real burden, one jumps on your back. You go on this way until you feel exactly the same as your stuckness.*

The purpose, now, is not to free yourself, but first to feel the energy stored in being stuck.

It is quite unlikely that you will stay in this state of being stuck for the rest of your life. Sooner or later it will transform into something else. But, from here, we can immediately go on to a second phase. Maybe you can feel in which direction the stored energy wants to flow. If your friends are still around you can try the following. Together with your friends go back again to that state of being immensely stuck. Someone is on your back while two others hold down your shaking arms that want to throw away all this stuff you have to deal with. Maybe a fourth one pushes papers, symbolising tasks to delegate, back into your hands.

The five of you have now made a field. You become, as it were, a group body, a kind of a system. Without words you attune to one another and, as a group body, you let the movement of being stuck transform. To what?... we'll see soon enough. Slowly the movement changes; the living picture that so beautifully showed your stuckness changes. Perhaps into another system or a new state. Into something that flows.

If you do this exercise several times, starting each time from the same point, you will be amazed at all the different changes of state that emerge.

You might even begin to appreciate being stuck. Seeing that it is the system that gets stuck and not just the individual. Getting stuck is almost impossible on your own. You get stuck into something. Into your work, into delegating, into writing a report... So what is actually getting stuck is already a system.

Getting stuck is a beautiful indicator, showing where you are deviating from what you want, from what the system wants from you, or from your destiny.

On a larger scale, an organisation or society that gets stuck is usually an indication that life-energy and joy are blocked somewhere in that system.

III.10 Trauma in organisations

Mary is Hungarian, 37 years old, a business woman. She is impeccably dressed. A woman of the world and she looks the part. She has worked in several multinationals, mostly organisations that combine elements of Hungarian, German and often another, for example American, business cultures. Currently she is managing her husband's installation company because he had to stop after a burn-out. She exudes strength.

When Mary begins to speak, she cannot be stopped. She begins with a big sigh, announcing that she finds this difficult to talk about. At this point I haven't a clue what 'this' might be. Then she says that something was triggered inside her when I spoke of how traumas tend to repeat on their anniversaries.

I feel the need to be careful with Mary and I offer her a lifeline. I ask her *"Is there any place where you feel safe?"* Her answer is *"No"*. This makes me even more careful. *"Is there someone here whom you would like to sit next to you?"* She points to a group member, whom comes and sits beside her.

Then the dam breaks and the flow starts and it is unstoppable. Mary tells us how she quickly climbed the ladder to become the marketing director in an international company. Everybody in the company seemed pleased. Then she relates how she was 'slaughtered' by a co-director. That is the word she uses, slaughtered. I am astonished, but get no chance to react. Mary gets a new job where, once again, she is soon successful, assuming an important position in a marketing department that wins a prestigious prize. Then she tells us how again a director summons her, gets a box of tin soldiers from a drawer, puts one tin soldier on his desk and says to Mary *"You see that tin soldier? That is you. And this is what I will do with you"*. And with a flick of his finger he knocks the tin soldier down.

And so she goes on for at least ten minutes. I know I must not interrupt her. To do so would be the same as what she is describing: cutting off what is growing, what is becoming. Finally she gets to her husband's installation company, the one she is managing now. She stops and looks at me expectantly. *"Oh, one more thing"*, she says, *"This happens every time I get a new job. After about two years, and always in March. This is really hard for me"*. The date is March 20th. Of course we all understand that this is about a trauma that repeats – as traumas seem to like doing. Why they repeat remains a mystery.

But traumas also seem to be mirrors for what is happening at various levels: the levels of society, of the organisation and of the individual.

Second movement by middlemanagement

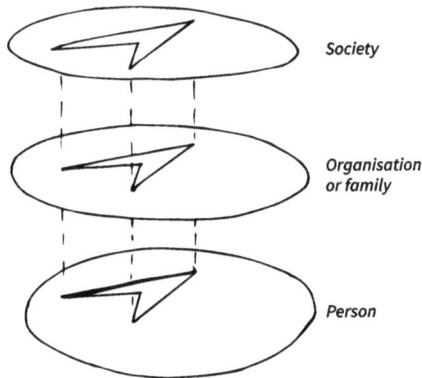

Society

Organisation or family

Person

Patterns repeat themselves at different layers

So I am wondering where we can start. I do not want to work on the personal trauma, because, today, we are working in an organisational context. We start at the abstract level, meaning the level of the pattern, trusting that we will learn what belongs at which level. Mary knows exactly what she wants to set up: the creator (someone who starts something new) and the executioner. Immediately, it's clear we are in the history between Hungary and Germany. It is clear that Mary has been 'taken into service' by a bigger field, a bigger pattern, that repeats itself. The pattern of the traumas between Hungary and Germany appears to have the same form as the pattern in Mary's professional life (and possibly the same as in Mary's internal system).

Slowly and carefully we peel off the layers. Slowly and carefully we place elements for the abilities that have been split off by the system, in order for the system to survive: the ability to bring something to an end, the ability to move freely and so on. Something else then needs attention: time. It is unclear in what time Mary is and if time is running at all. Actually, it seems as if time has stopped; the way clocks stopped in Japan at the moment of the 2011 earthquake. Where is the on/off switch for this trauma stopwatch? It appears to be with the victims of the original trauma. Only they seem able to give Mary permission for her clock to start ticking again. I know this sounds absurd, but I have often seen it in organisations. After an accident, or a business transfer or similar traumatic event it can seem as if the clock of that system has stopped. Often, the victims of the event are the only ones who can give permission for the world to turn again.

I ask Mary to say *"It is 2011. March the 20th, 2011"*. She cannot say it. Only when the 'original victims' have given Mary permission, can she say *"It is now the 20th of March... 2011"* and: *"after March comes April, then Easter, then May, then June."*

When I feel Mary's hands, they are cold. I comment about this and she replies *"Oh, but my hands are always ice cold"*. I take her back to the creator and the executioner, to the victims and to the different abilities that had to split off in order to survive. I ask her, jokingly, where the systemic heating is. She puts both her hands cross-wise on the heart of the creator and, eventually, the blood begins to flow again to her hands. At this point we have finished, at least for the moment. Processes of reconnection and completion have begun.

Trauma in bigger systems

We have known for a long time that people can become traumatised and that there are many ways to address this. But can a whole system become traumatised? Can a department become traumatised? Can a social field become traumatised, like a torn piece of silk?

A few years ago I started carrying those questions with me as I travelled. I found that not much was known about trauma in organisations, neither in the body of management literature nor in the world of systemic work.

From the experiences I collected during the last two years it seems quite likely that an organisation can become traumatised, and even long after the participants in the original trauma have left the organisation. It seems probable that one can do something about it and so prevent new traumas arising or the old trauma repeating.

What is trauma, exactly?

There are researchers and pioneers in the field of trauma who have collected models, definitions and insights that are helpful when considering trauma in organisations. We use the word trauma here, but actually it is not completely correct. Many events can have serious, potentially traumatic consequences, but whether or not they induce a trauma reaction is dependent upon the circumstances and the nature of the people or the system exposed to the event. So actually we need to differentiate between a potentially traumatising event and a trauma reaction. For the sake of convenience, we will use trauma in the context of companies, systems or people who suffer trauma reactions following a significant event.

Anngwyn St. Just is a trauma specialist, a lady, almost in her seventies, and a colleague of Peter Levine, another trauma specialist, who comes into the picture later.

Although they both worked for The University of California at Berkeley, they also have their own approaches to the issue of trauma, which complement each other. Anngwyn is more the systems thinker, while Peter tends to take a physiological perspective. Anngwyn knows systemic constellations well and uses them in her trauma work.

The third person laying these precious foundations is Franz Ruppert, a therapist and systemic constellations facilitator. The findings of Anne Ancelin Schützenberger are also important here.

Anngwyn St. Just

Anngwyn employs two criteria when describing trauma:

1. She calls it trauma when a system is so overwhelmed after an event, that the system does not spring back into its original state and strength. If the system does spring back, then she talks of a stressful or turbulent period.

2. She speaks of traumas in terms of broken bonds and connections. This tells us that a trauma is always systemic. Even when an individual gets traumatised, the effect is felt by family members, colleagues or other parts of the individual's system.

What follows is a striking example of how the trauma of one person cannot be isolated from the rest of the system. (This example did not arise out of an organisational context). Because of its clarity I want to mention it here.

A woman, of about thirty-five, came to a constellations workshop. She arrived in her wheelchair. I have seldom seen a person so complete. So I asked her "What are you here for?" "To thank the accident", she replies. When she was seventeen and helping to paint the family farm, she fell from a ladder, broke her back and had a spinal cord injury. When we do the constellation it is suddenly clear that for this woman, the accident brought about tremendous personal growth (The gift of the wound). But for her family and particularly for her mother, time stopped at the moment of the accident and so also did the development of the rest of the family members.

Peter Levine

Peter Levine noticed that when a lion jumps on an antelope, the antelope gets into a 'freeze' state when both the impulse to fight and the impulse to flee no longer function. The antelope falls down as if dead. Certainly the 'freeze' state protects against physical pain, as the organism shuts down to a degree. If the antelope survives the attack, it just shakes off the excess energy stored in the body. It quivers and shakes all over its body and then it continues its life. This energy release is necessary to continue a healthy life.

Imagine that you are a car where simultaneously the driver presses the gas pedal to the floor and steps fully on the brakes. You (the car) do not move, but inside you are full of turbulence and opposing forces. All this energy gets stuck in your body.

It seems as if people have lost their natural capacity for energy release. An interesting theory suggests that this is because we can get into our minds and dissociate when the ground becomes too hot under our feet. Animals cannot dissociate: they always live in primary emotions. So, after a trauma, for example, we have to do something specifically to get rid of the stored, stuck energy.

Two years ago I fell 50 meters down a mountain while hiking alone. The fall was completely unexpected. The path wasn't difficult, I was feeling good but probably missed my step, and then my heavy backpack did the rest. Immediately after the fall I was not sure I would survive. But after a complicated rescue mission and a stay in hospital I was back home again. Although I lost some of my scalp, tore my knee ligaments and had a lot of bruising inside and out, nothing essential was damaged.

Or so I thought. Later, when I found myself at the top of a staircase or a slope as steep as the one down which I had fallen, my body froze. It was very unpleasant. Especially as I felt that I couldn't handle these situations and feelings.

Systemic and therapeutic questions had ceased to help me. But what did help was the physiological method of Peter Levine. First, lifelines are put into place, and then you are taken slowly in the direction of the

---

trauma-event, but supported not to get into it again. This is the role and the art of the therapist and it requires a lot of skill. A good lifeline for me was the place in the garden, next to a little fire, where my wife and I like to sit and drink a glass of wine. There I feel safe and at home.

When the therapist first took me in the direction of the trauma-event my body started shaking uncontrollably. Skilfully she facilitated this movement in several small steps. The result of the first session was that I felt my legs were attached to my body again. The second session filled a little gap in my memory: the first quarter-second of the fall. That was a good feeling: my body no longer stiffened at the top of a staircase and fluid movement was possible again.

The importance of this energy release is to prevent your body freezing again in similar situations and to avoid generating a new accident. We all know people who seem accident-prone. You might wonder if they are experiencing a freeze situation just when they need to react quickly and appropriately.

Franz Ruppert

From Franz Ruppert came the insight about what happens inside a person when a traumatic event takes place. The personality splits into three main parts. There is a survival part that is directed at the survival of the organism. It prefers to deny the event as much as possible and ensures that if the organism survives, its reconstruction can start quickly.

I remember well that Bibi (my wife) and I were in a similar state after a miscarriage. "Be strong and get back to work as soon as possible". (Which was also the systemic sentence with which our parents dealt with World War Two.)

Then there is the split-off part. In order to survive, something splits-off in the person. For example the ability to make bonds and connections.

And there is still a healthy and healing (surviving) part that continues to function rationally.

Trauma

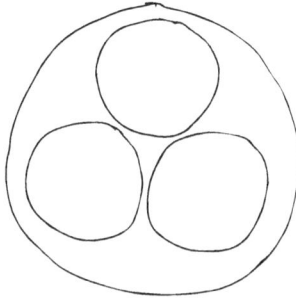

A system can react to a trauma by splitting itself up into multiple parts

After a trauma the inner parts of a person, that make him or her whole, are also separated. Inner bonds are broken; the inner system is torn apart.

From my research on trauma in organisations, it turns out that it is quite possible that a bigger system, for example a department, can show the phenomenon of splitting-off.

In a housing corporation, where people were dismissed because they did not share the new vision of the company, later generations of employees did not dare to commit their passion and vision to their work.

Anne Ancelin Schützenberger

Anne Ancelin Schützenberger is a historian who researched trauma in families over long periods of time, for example in the French royal family. This particular family was suitable for her research because it is a system that has been described in great detail for many generations. She found that traumas tended to repeat on anniversaries, and that traumas were repeated over the generations, even when it was impossible that a descendent could have known about the original trauma. Apparently, the trauma pattern is passed on in a way that does not use DNA, or conscious transmission. And, while we do not know how it works, we are sure in the knowledge that it does work.

In organisations too, we have noticed – several times now – that a trauma can repeat itself even when the current workforce and managers cannot possibly know about the original trauma.

Symptoms of trauma in organisations

Here are short descriptions of some of the symptoms and indications that have been discovered for trauma in organisations.

Unexpected an disproportionally resistance

Unexpected and disproportionally powerful resistance to a proposed change. What is actually happening here is a reactivation process. Reactivation is a normal phenomenon; an event suddenly triggers the repeat of an earlier trauma reaction, which can be biographical or systemic. Biographical means that the reactivated trauma occurred earlier in the professional life of a worker. For example, undergoing another merger, or being made redundant due to downsizing. A systemic reactivation means that the system 'remembers' something from an earlier trauma and the current employees, unconsciously, move into that field and experience the original trauma's reactivation.

Lack of trust

In the policy department of a pharmaceutical business in Brazil, the manager said that the department had gone crazy when the German parent company took over a Swiss pharmaceutical company. Although the takeover did not have a direct influence on the Brazilian department, an old pattern of deep mistrust between Switzerland and Germany surfaced in it. The symptom in this department was also the same, a sudden, non-specific, lack of trust.

Freeze state

Part of the organisation goes into the freeze state. Be especially attentive to the language that is used to describe the situation. If a manager speaks about a 'rigid organisation', listen to see if it is about a sudden rigidity, like water that suddenly freezes, or a slower, incremental process. The first case indicates trauma.

Time stops

Here again be attentive to the language that is used. For example: *"I entered the department and it was as if I had gone back twenty years".*

Absence of flow

There is no flow. Flow is not really possible when connections are broken. Listen carefully to see if it is more about flow that has dried up or flow that has been cut off abruptly. The first example is likely to be a drying up in the flow of giving and taking. The second example indicates trauma. In all these examples it is worthwhile to ask what happened in the organisation just before the flow was broken or before time 'stopped'.

No communication

There is no communication. The director of a building corporation said that the policy department, which handles contact with the municipality, simply could no longer communicate with it, for no apparent reason. "It is simply impossible!"

And again, try to feel or to find out if it is about communication that has been cut off or has dried up.

Repetition of traumas on the anniversary of an earlier trauma

I often ask how long an organisation has existed or when something in particular happened in the history of the organisation. Sometimes people know the exact dates or years, even if it is highly unlikely that people could know these facts so precisely. It is possible that knowing exact data is a part of the trauma. The director of the above-mentioned Brazilian pharmaceutical business said, without being asked, that the company had existed for 368 years. But he was talking about the European parent company and not the Brazilian office.

Trauma in an organisational constellation

In an organisational constellation, when we set up the most important elements of an organisational system, several of the above-mentioned trauma indicators become immediately visible. Here are two more:

Cold

If representatives in the constellation suddenly report that they feel ice-cold, or some of the observers feel cold or even the director, watching his 'own' organisation's constellation, has this feeling, then this is an indication of trauma. It's really quite logical. Trauma is partly a physiological reaction of broken connections and no flow. When the pattern is repeated in the bodies of those who are in contact with this trauma field, their blood flow stops. I am always very attentive to the person who brings in the question, to check if he suddenly turns white, because that means the blood flow to his face is being cut off. Difficulty with breathing is also an indication. One of the criteria I am attentive to, at the end of the trauma process, is if the representatives and the client have colour in their faces again and warm hands.

Spontaneous energy release

Sometimes in a constellation you see that a representative suddenly starts trembling and shaking uncontrollably. That can be energy release. When this happens I encourage the representative to allow it to continue. It has happened that the person who brought in the question also started trembling, even though in this particular case she had been a director for only two years and it was long after the traumatic event. A variant of energy release is that arms or legs of a representative suddenly want to move involuntarily. Again I encourage this to continue so that the movements can reach their destiny.

What helps?

How we can use constellations to heal trauma is becoming increasingly clear. There seem to be many possibilities to heal a traumatised field. To what extent those healing processes continue, after the constellation, is still the subject of research.

Recently a director brought the following question: "I have been the director of this organisation for a year or two now. We are too small to survive in the Netherlands and so we will have to merge in the near future. I would like to use a constellation to look at trauma in my organisation and I want to do whatever is in my power to heal those traumas before we start looking for a merger partner".

What a courageous step! It became clear that the healing process in the constellation gave her very useful information about what she could do, in and for her company, to prepare well for the impending change.

Let's take a trip through space and time in order to reassemble the split-off abilities and qualities of an organisation and to bring them back into the system.

A director of a nursing home feared that she had caused a trauma by leaving just before the home became involved in a merger process. She had left because she understood that she would not be the new director. It is true that the employees were traumatised, not by what she had done, but by the merger and how that had been conducted. However, the key sentence in the constellation, which the director (herself) said to the representatives for the employees was "I had the choice to leave.

You did not have this choice to move freely and so you also were cut off from your ability to move freely within the organisation". Then she chose a representative for the ability to move freely and brought that representative very slowly to the representatives of the employees. That was a slow and emotional process. But afterwards the representatives of the employees felt complete again and relaxed a little out of their rigid and frozen state.

When there are split-off parts, following a traumatising event in the organisational context, look especially for split-off abilities or qualities. Examples can be the ability to connect with your passion; the ability to be successful; the ability to speak out freely; the ability to be proud of a company name and so on. As a business manager you can easily locate those split off abilities. First you imagine yourself, for a moment, in the original traumatic event. Then you ask yourself in what ways did the traumatic event impact the employees. If their identities, as proud workers in the company, were taken away, future employees would not dare to feel pride in the name of the company. If their confidence in the management led to the unexpected sale of the company, then it is logical that future employees will have difficulties in trusting their direction.

Finding the original trauma

A director of a housing corporation, with whom we were doing a trauma process that did not feel totally complete, suddenly said: "Oh! This organisation is 94 years old and I remember stories that during the war a large number of our houses were bombed and many people died". Most of the audience felt shivers at this remark and so we knew that we had arrived at the original trauma. Offering security and safety was the ability that was lost here.

Permission

Getting permission to continue from the cut-off part or from the victims. There is a huge misunderstanding about mass redundancies. The misunderstanding is that the board can count upon the employees who remain to be so grateful so that they will be very motivated. This expectation is based on the principle of giving and taking: "*If you are allowed to stay, then you must accept that we offer you so much that we expect you, in return, to give us your loyalty, strength and productivity*". It appears that what really determines what happens is the principle everybody in a system has an equal right to have a place. The loyalty of the employees who remained employed is with those who were fired. From a place deep inside, the employees who were allowed to stay say "*Things will not be better for me than for you*". Many constellations have shown that permission to work well can come from those dismissed or from the victims of a traumatic event.

Acknowledgement

Recognising that the survival strategy at the time was the only possible strategy. In a downsized school department the remaining team members were so ashamed that each individual had gone into survival mode and had chosen only for themselves. This broke the bonds among colleagues. Recognising this strategy as the only possible one and the one that promised the team the best chance of survival, gave enormous relief and made it possible for the team members to look one another in the eyes again and reconnect.

Facing the traumatic event and growing bigger than it

A capable entrepreneur wonders why the businesses he starts all fail in some way. In the exploratory interview that follows, he suddenly remembers the bankruptcy of his grandfather's company. Through this he realises "Bankruptcy will always be a part of my businesses".

By integrating bankruptcy into the system and giving it a place, the whole system grows beyond the event – similarly to how a white blood cell grows larger by taking in undesired bacteria.

Allowing frozen situations to come to a natural end

Trauma often freezes movements and flow. In a constellation, if movements begin, encourage the representatives to continue the movements to their destiny. This repairs a pattern that confirms it is okay if movements in an organisation and movements towards society can, and are allowed, to reach their destiny. The same applies for flow. If tears begin to flow, and I do not necessarily mean tears of sorrow, just tears that could not flow, then let them flow. Also you often can hear people's stomachs begin to rumble and their intestines starting to work again: all are signs that flow and energy are moving again.

Permission to let the clock run again

In a constellation with the manager of a Latin American university's department for student support, the whole department was frozen. Nothing was possible. Suddenly the manager remembered that, some years earlier, a student was shot dead by the police during a protest on the campus. First the manager had to say to the representative of the dead student "The world has continued. Even after your death the world continued". *This returned life to the representative of the dead student who, in turn, was able to give permission to the present employees for time to begin again. The healing sentences were* "I cannot have a future. But I am glad that you can have one. It means my death was not in vain".

Prevention of reactivation

There are still more interventions or approaches for when it is the client who goes into the state of reactivation. This is more likely to occur when the client knows the trauma pattern from their own life or when there is a biographic trauma, or the combination of a biographical and a transgenerational trauma.

Offer sufficient lifelines

I learned from Anngwyn St. Just that many people, unconsciously, already wear, carry, or have at hand lifelines that can keep them in the here and now. Often in the form of jewellery, items or clothing of sentimental value, or remarkable personal attributes. Ask the client about the meaning of a specific lifeline-object of theirs. Often it is connected with a precious event or person. Then encourage the client to take this object in their hands as often as they want. Sometimes it helps to put a little distance between the client and the constellation by putting a chair between them or by symbolically creating a border by using a scarf. You can also invite another participant to sit next to the client as a lifeline. Or you can put an empty chair next to or behind the client to represent a precious person and/or resource.

Give them options

Let them choose. Keep telling the client that there are several possibilities and that the client may choose, each time, what the next step should be. One of the reasons a trauma reaction occurs is the fact that in the given circumstances there was no choice.

Do not interrupt the client during their story

Interrupting can cause the original trauma to be reactivated by cutting off the flow again. In constellations where there is no question of trauma, the client is often satisfied with the insights they receive. Then the client decides what he or she is going to do with the insights and we assume that the client is in a state where several options are possible and that the client is also in a state where they can take appropriate action. With trauma this is not so obvious. It strikes me that in trauma constellations in particular,

I allow all the time necessary for a healing movement to complete the process. Waiting until I'm sure flow has started again and the split-off parts are reintegrated.

Let the client take action himself in the final part of the constellation

This means more than just taking his or her place in the constellation. Especially with traumas, action was often impossible because the system had frozen. By letting the client take action herself in the constellation, a new pattern is created that contains the possibility to stay active when faced with trauma.

Split-off parts

Sometimes a split-off part of the client is unaware that the client has survived the trauma. In this case it is good if the healthy part of the system lets the split-off part know that the client has survived. In a trauma the events can be stored differently; often in another time order than how it really happened. For the process it appears not to matter. You can travel to and fro in space and time without a problem.

Concluding on prevention of reactivation: until now it has been amazing, and an enormous encouragement, to notice how down-to-earth businessmen and women, who have never seen a constellation, can easily co-operate in such a trauma-healing process. As I said earlier, we do not know yet what the longer-term effects are in the companies involved, although the general feedback is that such constellations are quite helpful.

Prevention of trauma

What can an organisation do, in general, to prevent trauma? Preventing trauma and its often far-reaching effects lies mostly in the hands of the management. Here are some possibilities.

Give people options

Research shows that the fewer the choices people can make, the more the trauma affects them.

Allow people to take action

Allow people to connect with their roots

Cultural, professional or other roots. It appears that people who can connect with their roots suffer less from traumatic events.

History

Look for traumas in the history of the organisation and give them a place, so that the organisation can continue to develop. When a traumatic event also had an effect on the local community, such as a fire in a company, a fatal accident or mass dismissal, then it is useful if the management recognises the event's effect on the outside world: *"We are that company where an explosion and fire occurred in 1972."* This helps to grow beyond the fire. Recently I saw a company that changed its name after a fire. As a local resident, this felt dishonest to me and did not affect my memories of the incident at all.

Recognise reactivation as early as possible and acknowledge it

In case of name change

In the case of a 'normal' change of name, it is important to respectfully recognise the former name and acknowledge how many people – clients, employees, suppliers and so on – were connected with this name. If a part of people's identities came from working for the company for a long time, give them that recognition. This helps prevent a part of their identities splitting-off when the company's name is discarded.

In case of mass dismissals

If there have been mass dismissals, 'the company' should visit the employees who were made redundant and their families and listen to their stories. Understand that dismissal can not only break the bond between employee and company, but also between the employee and their home or circle of friends. Perhaps the dismissal was worse for the family than for the employee himself.

Concluding on prevention of trauma: since our first cautious explorations into trauma in organisations, the theme has resonated in many countries. What I have described in this section are just the first steps on a, perhaps, rich and meaningful path.

III.11 Money

Some thoughts about money:

- Money obtained by effort tends to stay. Money obtained without effort, for example speculation, tends to evaporate.
- Money wants to be reinvested because it then serves society as a form of fuel or life-energy.
- Money has a particular 'quality'. It appears, for example, that it is impossible to accept a grant without also accepting the values of the grant provider.

We saw this, for the first time, in an Austrian institution that worked with the integration of asylum seekers. The institution had unexpectedly received a grant of one million euros. "The institution went crazy", said the policy manager, "completely bonkers, and we do not understand why". The constellation showed that it was not about the amount of the grant, but about the grant provider, who, so to say, seemed to be standing in the middle of the organisation and bossing the show.

At that moment the policy manager realised that, following the recent elections, the amount of the grant had been decided by the right-wing party, while before the elections it was decided by the left-wing party.

You also see this 'quality' with inheritances. Is the heritage being spent in a way of which the deceased would approve? Sometimes an inheritance requires the approval or the blessing of those who worked hard for it, before it can be put to use. This blessing does not always need to come from the one who bequeathed the inheritance.

Catherine has a problem with money, or more correctly, with large amounts of money. She cannot accept them. She is self-employed and really needs the money, but just can't take it. When the amounts of money get too large for her, she sees it as play money that she should tear up. Then her hand makes very powerful movements, like a slashing sword, unlike the soft and kind Catherine I'm used to. When I point out to her this slashing movement she has just made, she is totally unaware of it. This reminds of a trauma reaction. I just happen to have an envelope in my pocket containing a lot of money. As a test I put the banknotes on her lap. With a look on her face as if she has been stung by a wasp, she stares at the banknotes.

She has a family history in which a grandfather took money, which came from the grandmother's side, from his daughters and squandered it. This is not the first time I have seen money or property get lost when a son-in-law meddles with money from the female line.

Then I ask "How many people in your background had something essential cut off by money?" *She says* "Twenty". *We put up ten of them and seeing them touches Catherine. Most of them she knows by name. Then we ask the ten family members each to find a representative for that which was not possible for you anymore. Catherine is even more touched. In a long ritual she visits her family members who, one by one, look kindly at her when she asks for permission to handle money in a manner other than the ways with which she is familiar.*

Afterwards, she is able to keep the wad of banknotes in her hands and on her lap without a problem.

A little later, Janine comes to see me. She would like to keep this confidential. She has a problem. A man, with whom she had a short relationship, has given her € 700,000,--. She did not want to have his money, but he began transferring large amounts of money into her bankaccount. Then he left without a trace. Now she does not know what to do with the money.

Janine looks in her mid-thirties, very lively, sparkling and looks as if she could easily begin a chain of fashion shops. She tells how she used to be a drug addict. Later she found work in a hospital and now she has become a successful coach with an increasing number of business clients.

She used part of the money for her training. That felt appropriate. She does not feel the urge to buy a house, nor to buy luxury goods. She cannot give the money back, because the man left without a trace.

This sum of money the man gave to Janine makes the transaction seem strange.

I ask Janine "What 'problem' did the man solve by giving you so much money? In giving you the money, who did he see? You or somebody else?" *That resonates in her.* "You could do something with the money that serves those who paid a price for how this money was earned, or from whom this money came, even if you do not know them". *Then she nods with a serious look and begins to glow.*

- Now and then, a trend emerges to assess the value of services and products after they have been delivered and then to pay what accordingly. Experiences in the systemic field have shown us that this principle of paying according to how much you liked it does not work. By determining the value afterwards a judgement comes in. There is a strong indication that this judgement has the effect of getting the producer and consumer entangled rather than freeing them up for new transactions. It strikes me that the clearer the contract, the stronger the transaction.

Mostly money is representing something else. Sometimes it represents energy, sometimes values. Money is the carrier of those values.

When my wife and I thought about how much money we wanted to invest in a Volkswagen mobile-home, it appeared that the amount was related to our lifestyle. For us, being independent is an important value. Even if we had spent a lot more than we actually did, we would have bought a vehicle that would not have felt comfortable for us. The second-hand mobile-home we bought matches our lifestyle perfectly. It feels more second home than second hand and we spend at least two months a year in it. We'd rather invest (the difference) in solar panels, and be even more autonomous, than buy the latest model.

In Latvia, one of the small Baltic states, a project leader from the ministry of finance came with an issue. Latvia is about to change their currency from the Lats to the Euro. The project leader wanted to know what actually was the real meaning of the resistance against the conversion to the Euro. Historically, Latvia had enjoyed only short periods of independence. The Lats was very identified with the values of independence. The Euro was identified with the values of taking opportunities and progress. By experiencing this and understanding this deeper meaning of the Lats, the project manager got many ideas about how to facilitate the conversion process.

III.12 Trust

In this chapter we explore trust, distrust and their breeding grounds in organisations.

Many business transactions originate with eye contact and are agreed with a handshake. Every language knows the saying 'a man's word is his bond'.

Often, when I am invited to work for a big organisation, the most essential part of the contract is concluded in the first seconds that I meet the person in charge. Usually it goes without words. Then, in a manner of speaking, the client and I stand shoulder-to-shoulder.

Call it trust, or whatever you want.

Such a source of trust can be rooted in the person, in the organisation, the line of business or in society. These sources of trust or lack of trust can jump from one layer to another, or resonate with each other.

An example, originally written as a blog entry at the end of a visit to Uruguay.

Uruguay, December 2011. Vartan is a tall guy with quite a lot of black hair, combed backwards. His business trades in engine parts. He fired his last-remaining employee after seeing the employee, on the closed-circuit TV, overcharging clients and pocketing the difference. "My heart is not in the company anymore. I want to become a therapist or social worker. I've been trying to sell the business, but each time, one way or another, the sale falls through. Why does this happen?" A bit later he says "I used to be one of the best in this market with a good reputation and business was flourishing. Lately, however, the market has been flooded with black market and stolen parts".

In no time the elements of trust and distrust loom up. It is touching when Vartan looks at his business with tears in his eyes and says that he has never cheated a client. His personal guiding principle of honesty and straightforwardness is attacked on all sides by theft and mistrust, both in the market and in his company. Vartan realises now that he is facing a difficult choice: closing his business down and keeping his honour and guiding principles, or selling his business with the likelihood that it will be sacrificed to guiding principles that are not in line with his. We leave the choice to him…

Buyers are able to feel the guiding principles of the business in which they are interested. What will they do with the principles? You can't buy the business and not the guiding principles. Perhaps a stronger decision would be to inwardly acknowledge that you are actually buying the guiding principles and getting the business as part of the deal. Goodwill, so to say, from a systemic perspective.

Seldom, in one day, have I met the words trust and distrust so often in a workshop as here in Uruguay. A group of extremely kind but also quite sceptical people. Aha, there you have it again, distrust wrapped up in scepticism. The organisers thank the participants for their trust; they even thank me for my trust in coming to Uruguay.

Although I have been here for a short time only, Uruguay seems an incredibly open and prosperous country. It has a strong left-wing government with a president who walks to the neighbourhood café for lunch and tends to his garden in his free time. The state is strong and so are its social programs. The middle class used to be the biggest class until the crisis of 2003. Now the gap between rich and poor has become much bigger again. Montevideo is kind of a big village. Everybody knows everybody. The husband of Anna, one of the organisers, greets me warmly in Dutch. As a 22-year-old, at the beginning of the military dictatorships in Argentina and Uruguay, he fled to the Netherlands. There he lived, studied and worked for eight years.

Over a glass of wine we talk about the dictatorship of 1973 – 1985. Linnea, another organiser, talks about how awful it was. How, on the way to school, you could never stop to chat in threes or fours, because you would be seen as conspirators and your parents ran the risk that their children would be picked up and never seen again. It had already struck me, several days earlier, that people here, in contrast to other American-Latin countries, do not stand or walk in little groups. I ascribed that in the first instance to their feeling for individuality and autonomy. But now I know the real reason…

The man who became president after the dictatorship was imprisoned in a hole in the ground for eight years. When he came out of it he said "Terrible mistakes have been made. But I do not feel like bringing the perpetrators to justice; the soldiers, the army. That would be revenge rather than justice and then we would be no better than them".

In several referenda, all three million Uruguayans let it be known that they do not want the military to be judged. The new military leaders suggested that investigation, openness and judgement within their own organisation would take place. When I ask how perpetrators and victims get along in this 'big village', Linnea says that much is still secret

and that people keep their mouths shut. Anna adds "Although reconciliation is in the air and is proposed everywhere and acknowledged
as the best strategy to grow beyond good and bad, it is still too early.
The wound is still open".

In one of the constellations, in which two partners in a business want
to get rid of a third person, I run into an invisible wall… indeed, it is too
early.

*A week ago when the site of an army barracks was excavated, the body
of a much-loved teacher was found. He had been tortured horribly and
everybody was convinced he had been innocent of any 'crime'. Suddenly, with this, something broke. Now there is a call for 'justice'.*

How, oh how, do the wounds of civil wars heal?

Trust, from a systemic point of view, has to do with the main systemic
principles of order, belonging, balance in taking and giving, and destiny.

When you stay in your rightful place in the order, you are trustworthy,
in the sense of being predictable and reliable.

Related to the balance in taking and giving, when you trust someone,
you give him or her a part of yourself, so creating a strong, sometimes
symbiotic relationship. Like trusting your money to a bank. You do not
just give them your money, you also give them a part of yourself, called
'trust'. The effect of betrayal is that you are cut of from the part of yourself
you gave to someone else. You need to take this part back before you can
trust again.

From the perspective of belonging, trust means that the other person,
the one who you are trusting, grants you the right to belong. You become
part of the same tribe.

From the perspective of destiny, trust means to accept in an active way
what comes to you from the emerging future. Trust here also means to
walk together with someone else (my bank, for example) in the same direction, facing the emerging future. Trust here does not mean: I will sit on
the couch while you walk, while you face the future.

"To take, however it comes…" was a favourite expression of my father and his mother, my grandmother… and my father lived that way, and he also died that way.

III.13 The contract

Tadeus owns a business providing services to support the well-being of employees in large companies. He uses a number of freelance physiotherapists, whom he hires on short-term contracts to work in these companies. Tadeus also contracts directly with those companies. Now Tadeus's problem is that the physiotherapists feel more connected to the companies than to him. Even more annoying is that when their contracts expire, the physiotherapists take Tadeus to court because they see that there is still a lot of work and money to be earned in those companies. They accuse him of unfair dismissal.

Ok, we are in Brazil where employees often take legal action but, according to Tadeus, this happens to him far more often than the average.

He looks at me with his warm kind eyes and asks "Why do they do that?". The 'why' question keeps me puzzled for long time. Would Tadeus be helped by an answer to this 'why' question? Or is something else needed? After a while I ask him "Are you too kind?" "Yes" he says, "and I do have a paternalistic attitude".

A short constellation shows that the client companies fascinate the physiotherapists. I ask Tadeus to find his own place in the constellation, as the entrepreneur that he is. He stands next to the physiotherapists, just as obsessed by the clients as are the physiotherapists. Moreover he feels much smaller than these companies. It is clear that the physiotherapists will take all the room they can get.

Then I ask Tadeus to stand shoulder to shoulder with the representative for the companies. He notices a feeling of power rising in him. He seems to be able to manage this. From there he says to the physiotherapists "Your contract has a beginning but it also has an end. If you want to work here, it is one of the conditions. Take it or leave it".

Then Tadeus realises that a contract does not help if you are not strong enough to set the conditions without a contract. A contract reinforces a

relationship but cannot replace a weak relationship. Small print is fine,
but it works only once. The customer, once trapped by the small print,
will know better than to accept the contract a second time, unless the
contract is, in reality, worthless to everybody.

Agreeing the start date for a contract is not so difficult. But setting an end date asks a bit more. When agreeing a contract it is important to connect with its end. To know and feel that the day will come when it will be over. Beginnings tend to have far more energy than endings. In Tadeus's case, there is also an order to the contract creation. The contracts with the client companies become the frameworks for the contracts with the physiotherapists.

Contracts demand that you take full responsibility for negotiating and agreeing them. It weakens you when you feel unsatisfied and begin to complain like a little child, pointing to your contract as the child might to his big brother. Even if you win your battle, and a court enforces the contract, it is likely to be a Pyrrhic victory.

III.14 Delegating

An owner of a small business tells me that when she tries to delegate
tasks to her employees they leave the company. Her business has po-
tential and its growth gives her, as the owner, more and more work to
do: too much to do all by herself.

A constellation quickly makes it obvious what the problem is. The man-
ner in which she delegates work invites others into her circle of influence.
Invites them to remain there, or even to take over her role. This weakens
the whole system.

But how do you delegate in a way that actually strengthens the system? You should give tasks to an employee from a position of strength. This might seem paradoxical: you think that delegating the task is what will make you feel stronger. So, must I feel strong before I begin to delegate? Indeed! Each function, each role in a company, is a mini-system in itself, which needs a certain amount of inherent strength in order to ensure the clarity and autonomy of the position, and to ensure that the holder feels comfortable in the role. If, for example, your role becomes too much for you, simply because there is too much work for just one person, you must take care that delegating does not erode the autonomy of your role. If you appoint a deputy-director, ensure that when you transfer the tasks, you do not transfer (and this way undermine) your role as director. The same is true for departments.

In an international organisation, where there was a pattern of sexual intimidation, a department was charged with handling the sexual harassment issue. Literally 'charged', because the management was not prepared to face this issue. By 'delegating' their responsibilities to the department in this way, the management undermined themselves.

Delegating can be seen as creating mini-functions that you assign to an employee. As we saw earlier, it is important to create those mini-functions from a strong position and only then to hand them over. If you want to appoint a manager to take over some of the responsibilities of the owner, first you must 'clean up' the organisation.

Delegating from a feeling and position of strength, gives focus and growth.

Delegating from a sense of being overwhelmed, weakens the organisation and creates doubt inside and outside.

III.15 Licences

Two women have a company with a lot of potential. Jeanet is the founder and developed the business concept. Carla joined 9 years later.

They have done constellations, twice, around questions about growth, about the structure of the organisation and about the division of income. After the second constellation Jeanet wrote me a letter, with another question, this time about the division of licensing fees. For both of them this issue raised questions about equality and justice. Their business is about a special form of consulting. Jeanet has developed the idea and the consulting models. Both Jeanet and her colleague Carla, by working with these models, create new knowledge. They have placed their work in two companies: an exploitation company, where they apply their model in their consulting practice and, what they call, a 'knowledge' company. The income from this knowledge company comes from the licence fees professionals have to pay to use this consulting model after being trained. Another part of the income of this knowledge company comes from booksales. The question is about this knowledge company. Basically Jeanet's concern is that she wants to be the main or only shareholder of this company, because she feels that 'to be my right'.

My reaction and some reflections follow:

"Hello Jeanet and Carla,"

Knowledge wants to be shared. We cannot own knowledge, although all kinds of copyrights and so on suggest otherwise. When knowledge flows it generates money. Knowledge can be picked up by others in a good way, enriched and be used, as you and your students do. It can also be 'stolen': when others run away with what you have developed without asking you, without respecting you or crediting you as the source.

Personally, I have encountered both: people respectfully developing 'my' ideas further and people running away with 'my' ideas as if they were the source.

I consider knowledge as shareware, but I find it reasonable to get back something for all those years of pioneer work. Whether or not it is a co-incidence that you originally developed your concept and not Carla, does not matter much: there is only one pioneer and that is you.

The trainers I engage and who pass on my hard-earned knowledge, earn less than me and they hand over a part of their fees to our institute (and so to me). How much is a matter of what feels right to us all. We revisit these arrangements at least once a year. There is no justice but there is reasonableness.

In your letter you mention justice a lot, but actually that does not exist. Because what authority would decide what is right? One that is outside of the organisation which you formed together. You could consult such an authority about what is right and fair, but would that be beneficial to working together? It is much easier to keep a balance of reasonableness between each other, than to depend upon outside intervention.

So I cannot give you a concrete answer about what would be right. You have to work it out together, where you, Jeanet, as the initiator, are a kind of ultimate decider and Carla has the same possibility as a colleague would have. You are responsible for what you do and decide as initiator and Carla for what she does and decides as your business partner. As long as you, Jeanet, keep contributing to the development of this method, it seems to me that the fact that you are nine years ahead of Carla is expressed by the difference in the division of the licence fees. If a time comes when you cease to contribute so much to the development and Carla begins to contribute more, then you could both receive the same amount for a while. If Carla develops a new branch, direction or model, then of course she would get a bigger share of the licence fees, reflecting her greater contribution to the knowledge base. If you slow down, and Carla keeps acquiring new knowledge, then you, as the originator, get an agreed and reasonable share of the licence fees and Carla receives a larger share than you – if she continues renewing the method.

"*Kind regards,*

Jan Jacob"

Roughly there are two models to handle knowledge acquisition. One model suggests that you cannot own knowledge, even knowledge that you developed or discovered. In this model you are seen as a source from which the knowledge does not come from you but, just like a mountain spring, flows through you. According to this model others can 'refresh' themselves, gaining nourishment from the knowledge and adding their own insights and learning to the knowledge base. Becoming, in their turn, also a source. This model accelerates knowledge acquisition. Individuals are recognised as the original sources of knowledge, but also for their incremental contributions to what is known. It is a centrifugal model where knowledge is not contained in the centre, but becomes widely available and is in service of society.

Income derives from how you apply the knowledge and by bringing it to the attention of interested parties in such a way that they want to pay you for it. If others surf on the wave of 'your' knowledge and insight, it is understandable – in the balance of giving and taking – that, for an appropriate and limited period, you are rewarded. Responsibility for verifying the accuracy and relevance of such knowledge lies not only with the founders but also with society. In this open system the knowledge exposes itself to society to be tested against current criteria. It puts the responsibility firmly with the clients for identifying if the knowledge is correct and relevant to them.

The other model is that you can own knowledge and, when you own something, you can sell or lease it. Usually this needs a system of licensing or franchising, and a supervisory authority that manages the process and maintains and guards the quality of the knowledge. This is a more centripetal model and allows control and monitoring of the knowledge acquisition. New knowledge is gained more slowly in this model.

I cannot say which model is better. But I can say that I feel more at ease with one of these models. However, my level of comfort probably depends on precisely what kind of knowledge is involved.

For pre-existing knowledge, that already exists in human society – such as systemic knowledge – and so, in principle, already available to everyone like the air we breathe, the first model seems the most appropriate to me. Furthermore it supports rapid and sustainable development and propagation via a wide range of applications.

And if that development ceases after a time?

Then, apparently, the knowledge acquired is no longer sufficiently relevant to find a connection in society. And then it is good that it stops.

Licence and Patent

It is maybe useful to make distinction between a licence and a patent. A licence is more about providing knowledge and being paid for it. With a patent it is more about establishing the right to make, use or sell a 'concrete' invention. That product or invention is the solidification of the knowledge, not the knowledge itself.

My older brother, who has started many businesses, is currently busy developing, making and erecting Mongolian tents. He derives his great-

est satisfaction from applying, in a modern context, the ancient knowledge and experience of the people who developed those tents to survive on the steppes of Mongolia. After an earthquake in Pakistan and the need for shelter in the severe winter cold in remote, ruined mountain villages, my brother developed a tent that could be dropped from a plane without the risk of it being damaged and without the need for a helicopter (There are very few helicopters in that part of the world). My brother incorporated all his know-how and experience into that tent, which excelled in its stunning simplicity and effectiveness. It would be relatively simple for my brother to patent that tent, but he couldn't patent the knowledge contained within it. That belongs to everyone who contributed to it, particularly the nomadic peoples of Central Asia and others who used that knowledge respectfully.

Systemically it seems often difficult to obtain a patent in a good way. Sometimes larger forces are at work. For example, when the time is ripe for a specific innovation, often we see it appear simultaneously in several places. This seems to be what happened with the art of printing, some centuries ago. Apparently, in service of something bigger, the evolution of society, it was time for printing to be 'invented'. I wonder… when is a patent more in service of the inventor or more in service of society?

I remember very well the constellation of an inventor who was considering submitting a patent application for an invention of his. Via the constellation it became clear to him that if he pursued a patent application he risked losing his qualities as an inventor. That was too high a price for him.

" *Copyright means 'Copy it Right'* **"**

Robert Dilts

In other words: 'with respect and mentioning the source'.

III.16 The success-inhibition script

"Earning money is easy for me, but I just can't seem to keep it" *sighs a pleasant-looking woman in her early fifties.*

Another says "I don't seem able to earn money doing the work I like doing, and for which I am appreciated by my peers in the international art trade".

A man says "I am good at starting-up businesses, but each time they look like being financially successful, I quit the company".

"*Oh, you mean a pattern like this?*", I ask, while making this drawing on a flipchart or in the air with my hands.

Second movement by middlemanagement

Pattern of a success-limiting script

I've noticed, during workshops, that this often brings people suddenly to the edge of their seats.

I call this the success-inhibition script. Success is approaching, the business is flowing and growing, income is on the increase… and then suddenly something 'happens' or you 'do' something, which causes the business to start going downhill, fast.

For people and companies experiencing this, the frustrating thing is not just that they do not want it to happen, but that they do not understand why it is happening. The second question is often even more pressing than the first one.

Consciously or unconsciously this is usually a very familiar pattern for them. Often it helps to reassure them by pointing out that, in spite of the pattern, they are still able to earn money in some way.

"But exactly what causes it?" she muses. *"My friends and colleagues can't give me a clue either."*

So... for what is this pattern a solution?

With whom would you become unequal or to what would you no longer belong if you would be and stay successful? Who, in your background, was not allowed to taste the miracle of success? Sometimes in this work, you come upon brothers or sisters whom fate has treated badly. Looking systemically, their (heavy) fate can revisit any family member at any time, but in your family it struck your older brother. Deep inside you can feel that it could, just as easily, have struck you. There is already an uneven distribution in the family, and, not from reason, but from somewhere deep inside our whole being, we do not want this to become even more unfair.

Who paid a high price so that this family could survive, become rich or simply could do well? A classic example of this phenomenon is slavery. Slaves paid the price for the wealth of plantation owners. Inside such a system there was a dynamic equilibrium between perpetrators and victims. If they remained caught in that dynamic then it might be that, many generations later, a businessman or woman or even a whole family is still maintaining this equilibrium... and the sawtooth 'ritual' is born: alternating periods of perpetrator and victim. Maybe it helps to realise that losing your wealth during those periods when you are (unconsciously) identified with victimhood is a mild form of being taken into the service of loss. In similar situations, some people lose their lives.

There is something else to consider with this master-slave dynamic, that continues to be visible as a general, unconscious picture in many organisations. It is possible to remain trapped in this dynamic, even when you are aware of this pattern, where one feels 'the slave' and the other 'the master'. People who are against authority or allergic to hierarchy, are actually trapped in this dynamic. This being against hierarchy, however understandable this might be, is a good way to maintain the polarity dynamic of perpetrator-victim.

But we should understand that, originally, there also was a form of co-creation or mutual gain: masters provided slaves with protection, food and a form of security. How is it that a handful of Spaniards, in 16th century Mexico, were able to subdue the Indian cultures within two years? Maybe the reasons do not lie only with the conquistadores. Perhaps there was something in the Indian peoples that agreed with these larger forces. It is more about an inner attitude of being connected through such a dynamic and how that counteracted any desire to erase the horrible deeds and events that accompanied the dynamic. As soon as both parties recognised that they kept each other in balance, needed each other, each had their part, then it became possible to look each other straight in the eyes and grow beyond the pattern: to create respect and a new society.

It is remarkable how in Uruguay the ex-members of the military dictatorship are more willing to give information to the left wing parties about what happened, than to the conservative parties. The military, and the leftist political movement who previously manifested themselves in (amongst others) the Tupamaros movement, respect each other, see each other clearly and are bound to each other. This shared respect allows the emergence of a new society without calls for revenge and trial. Perhaps then the sawtooth process will stop.

More recipes for experiencing the sawtooth

Who used to live in your house? Did anything happen on the site of your company's factory or offices, or in the geographic area from which you now make your profit? It has been known for a long time that the energy of far-reaching events – battlefields, deportation, abuse, murder and so on – attaches to buildings and areas. 'Stolen goods do not thrive' is popular Dutch folk wisdom and it looks as if this can reach across many generations. What was stolen from whom and, crucially, never acknowledged?

Once I was with a group that visited a spiritual centre in Mexico, built on ground that had been stolen from the original inhabitants and, in the building process, part of a mountain had been excavated. The spiritual centre looked wonderful, but it had a really unpleasant effect on us visitors. Only when we withdrew about one hundred meters from it were we able to breathe freely again.

One of the most touching cases I encountered in this context concerned a large group of people in Vladivostok, who came with the question "Do we have the right to be here at all?" The city of Vladivostok began life, in the late 19th century, as a military base.

Now that the military function of this harbour, once the biggest fortress in the world, is gone, the inhabitants of this large town are very concerned about finding a new identity and ways to make a living. An anthropologist and a sociologist talk about all the different tribes who lived in this area over the last millennia and buried their dead in this soil. When such a tribe was forced to leave the area after being conquered by another tribe, they had to leave their dead ancestors behind. The constellation suggested that permission to flourish, for the present inhabitants of Vladivostok, should come from the dead of the expelled former tribes. Seeing this, about eighty Russians in the room were moved to tears.

The sawtooth: recognising an outstanding debt and recognising both sides of the coin of gain and loss. Accepting that this world knows, so well, the forces of both perpetrator and victim. Integrating these opposing forces offers a possibility to grow beyond being trapped in the pattern.

III.17 Downsizing

What is downsizing from a systemic perspective? We often see downsizing as unpleasant and negative. Downsizing appears to be the opposite of growth. Apparently, if growth stops, we must be doing something wrong.

Although we all know that a system or an organisation or an economy cannot endlessly expand, if only because Earth's resources are limited, there is always somewhere the desire for, and the belief in, growth.

Downsizing is usually bad news: an announcement that times will not be so good for a while, that you'll be doing more work with fewer colleagues and wondering if you might be next in line for the chop. Apparently we are more attracted to and focussed on growth than we are prepared to accept, let alone embrace, downsizing.

This example came from a colleague of mine:

Some years ago I took on an independent advisory role in a major educational institution. It was in a part of the Netherlands where the population was in decline. In a talk with a member of the executive board of this institution, I was struck by the strength of his involvement. He told me: "In our schools the pain of the cutbacks can be felt; almost every family is affected. This is a clear consequence of reducing the number of pupils as well as teachers. As a director I am quite worried about it".

From this example you can see that downsizing causes places in the system to be no longer occupied. Literally, there are empty seats in a classroom where pupils used to sit. This hurts the teachers and pupils who are still there. For how long will the hope or illusion exist that those places once again will be filled?

Clearly stating what is, although painful, is what heals. *"Those places will never be occupied again"*. Facing-up to reality makes the pain intense but, thankfully, short-lived. If society attaches to hope or illusion, the whole system easily goes into secondary feelings and inner images that want to bring back the past. Downsizing requires the courage to face what is.

Growth and decline are natural processes. With each breath our chest rises and expands, falls and contracts. In nature growth and decline interchange with day and night, with the seasons and the climate. Growth and decline are adaptive responses to changing circumstances. Populations grow and decline.

Darwin introduced the idea that growth is a battlefield. The best-adapted species survive at the expense of the less-adapted species. So decline indicates less or less-effective adaption or, more simply put, failure.

In the middle of the last century the DNA discoveries made by Watson and Crick proposed some new ideas: the DNA in the cell nucleus determines all the possibilities for the cell and so also for the (eventual) living being. Sometimes mutations cause anomalies in the DNA with unfavourable outcomes for the species. But, just now and then, there appears a favourable mutation and then the species evolves a little step further. Evolution as a permanent lottery. Growth means, then, to increase not only in number, but also in development. However, most images of downsizing depict it as the opposite of development; more like coming to a complete stop.

Gradually it becomes clear that the story of evolution is more complex, and maybe is even completely different, than what has been thought for centuries. How does a newly-divided young cell, still undifferentiated, know what it must become? This remains one of the great mysteries of biology. Does the DNA determine it? No! It appears that the environment determines if a cell becomes a muscle cell or liver cell, for example. Placed in a muscle the stem cell becomes a muscle cell; placed in the liver a liver cell. The impulses from outside, from the rest of the system – or call it the field – determine how the cell will develop. The intelligence of the cell is in the cell membrane, the thin film around the cell containing receptors that are extremely sensitive to the cell's environment. The DNA here is not the 'brain' of the cell, but the reproduction unit. Bruce Lipton describes this, at length, in his book The Biology of Beliefs.

Research has shown that DNA not only mutates spontaneously, but also changes in response to external stimuli. A whole new branch of research is developing: epigenetics.

Why are we talking about it here, in a book about organizations and in a chapter about downsizing? This is about the images we have about phenomenon's such as evolution and growth, decline, downsizing and decay. For ages there was an accepted model in which life was directed by the nucleus, which caused changes to take place. But the newer images of evolution reflect an almost opposite process: from the environment or the field, the individual – from cell to whole organism – is formed and directed. These images are, of course, an immediate threat to existing concepts such as the feasibility of society, the primacy of free will and the possibility of continuous growth.

Back to downsizing: systems do not care much about what happens in society or what society thinks. Downsizing is a natural process of reacting to a changing environment. Downsizing is then an action rather than the result of being a victim of circumstance. Downsizing means being in contact with society via all the system's senses; feeling what is happening and what needs to be done in the organisation. Downsizing means being completely attuned to the movements of the spirit-mind, even when it asks for you to surrender. But, in that surrender, doing what is needed without losing strength. In this sense downsizing is not failure, but a sign of life force.

I want to give two examples of organisations that had to downsize and how, through the downsizing process, some surprising insights emerged about showing that the process was really about the guiding principles of the organisation.

Twenty years ago a handful of idealistic people formed an association for social empowerment in the Basque country. They have grown into an institution, employing 400 people, that has an enormous effect on how Basque society develops. Now, suddenly, they are confronted with the spectre of downsizing; fewer people and less funding. The director says that it isn't too bad, that the downsizing in one sector will be compensated by growth in another sector and that he has many ideas for new projects. The HR manager sees it quite differently. Perhaps because she actually has to carry out the downsizing, to do the dirty work. After an evening of good-natured arguing they decide to look at their question via a constellation. Something soon becomes clear: the guiding principle of this institution has always been. There is a place for everybody. Initially this meant for each person in Basque society. But, quietly and gradually, this has also become the guiding principle inside the institution... There is a place for every employee. Then the penny drops: downsizing is so hard to accept because it means a direct attack on their guiding principles. This applies to downsizing in society just as much as it does to downsizing in their own institution. It feels like a new guiding principle is arising, something like 'Accept your responsibilities'. In the case of the director and his HR colleague, this means facing the consequences of the changes in the society and acting accordingly. Actually that was exactly what the good-natured argument, over a beer in that cosy Bilbao pub, was about: the HR manager had tried to convince the director that everyone had to open their eyes and see the changes occurring around and outside them. The director still found this difficult.

With this new guiding principle of 'taking responsibility', downsizing suddenly looked different: now it offered the possibility to reinforce the strengths of the institution rather than undermine it. Seen this way, downsizing in this institution became a stimulus for systemic growth.

A Spanish enterprise, part of a German multinational company, had enjoyed continuous profit for over 30 years, but had made a loss in each of the last 3 years. The Spanish owners did not want to face up to these losses. The German company was founded during the war and the Spanish company later. Suddenly I ask the consultants of the Spanish company "Was it thirty years of profit or thirty years of victory?" "Victory", *is their soft reply.* "It was always about conquering other countries and our competitors. The owners are more like brothers in arms than business partners. If you live from the image of war then it is difficult to face loss". *In this particular case downsizing could be felt by the owners as loss of honour. It is easier to feel unconcerned than to lose face.*

These insights helped the consultants to consider if there might be downsizing metaphors that would be more helpful for the company?

While a business is growing: becoming bigger, attracting more clients, fulfilling more orders, purchasing more equipment and taking on more employees, it is good, already, to be in contact with possible downsizing. That keeps the system focused. Then the leader knows that if he is strong enough to grow the company, he is also strong enough to downsize the company. All the employees feel that as a supporting force. Systemically seen, it is strange if a director leaves when growth ceases and another director comes in to handle a downsizing or reorganisation. Then you split up the natural process of expansion and contraction into two separate processes and possibly into two separate companies.

Guiding an organisation through a time of downsizing asks, perhaps, for a more loving attitude than guiding in times of expansion.

Looking ahead

After a crisis and downsizing comes a period of growth again, but perhaps in an unfamiliar form.

Because the situation is often completely new, we are confronted with something we do not know and cannot know yet and, at first encounter, might not even recognize as growth.

Something similar might happen with the development of systemic work: growth or development in a direction we do not yet know or can anticipate.

What force or need will take systemic work into its service? What new forms will it take? Will it evolve more in the direction of social questions? Is systemic work, per se, meant to add meaning to society or is it being deployed increasingly to that end?

Or will it decline and return to its essence and reflect if its destiny has been achieved?

I do not know the answers and I watch the developments with an open heart.

Sources

To write this book I drew on far more sources than I can mention here. So I have chosen to limit the list to the most important sources and those mentioned specifically in the text. I have not provided a classic, detailed bibliography: I assume that the interested reader can find the necessary details easily via the Internet.

The substantial group of people who brought cases for constellations, or questions about their organisations, formed an important source. A number of those cases became examples in this book. I changed the names of those involved. Many thanks to them and to the following people for their help in bringing this book to fruition.

Bert Hellinger

Most important source and mentor in the field of systemic phenomenological work. Recommended reading: *Success in Life and Work Movements of the Spirit-mind*.

Gunthard Weber

Gunthard opened up the field of systemic work in organisations. Founded a number of organisations around systemic work that gave many people access to the philosophy and practice of systemic work.

Insa Sparrer and Matthias Varga von Kibéd

Co-developed structural constellations and contributed significantly to our understanding of the underlying principles of systemic phenomeno-logical work.

Albrecht Mahr

One of the pioneers in the area of political constellations. From his web-site (www.mahrsysteme.de) you can download a number of his articles including *Das Wissende Feld* (The Knowing Field).

Rupert Sheldrake

Biochemist; studied at Cambridge University, England and Harvard University, USA. First to assert the existence of morphic fields. *A New Science of Life: The Hypothesis of Morphic Resonance*.

Lynne McTaggart

Science journalist; books include The Field: *The Quest for the Secret Force of the Universe* (2003) and *The Bond: Connecting through the Space Between Us* (2011). Her investigation into the scientific research around quantum physics, evolution theory and cell biology connects well with certain of the concepts explored in this book.

Bruce Lipton

Biologist in the new field of epigenetics. Wrote *The Biology of Belief*, which proposes the idea that genes and DNA are affected by 'their' environment – which includes one's thoughts and emotions. He makes the switch in thinking from centrally controlled systems to systems controlled by the environment.

Thomas Latka

Philosopher, specialising in topology. Articles include *Feld* (Field). Personal exchanges have been extremely valuable to my understanding of how to work with the phenomenon of the Field.

Otto Scharmer

Developed Theory U, a process for essential change in organisations and society. For summaries, articles and new developments visit:
www.presencing.com
Recommended: *Theory U: Leading from the Future as It Emerges* (2009).

Arawana Hayashi

Translated the transitions in the U-process (of Theory U) into movements. Through her workshop *Embodied Presence: Art of Making a True Move*, she facilitates experiential contact with the developmental steps of Theory U.

Anngwyn St. Just

Pioneer in the field of social trauma.
Recommended: *A Question of Balance: a Systemic Approach to* Understanding and Resolving Trauma (2009).

Peter Levine

Developed Somatic Experiencing, an approach to personal trauma therapy. Recommended: *Waking the Tiger: Healing Trauma* (1997).

Anne Ancelin Schützenberger

French psychologist, invented the term psychogenealogy and wrote the bestseller *Aie, mes aîeux!* (see below for English title) in which she describes the repetition of patterns through several generations. *The An-*

cestor Syndrome: Transgenerational Psychotherapy and the Hidden Links in the Family Tree (1998).

Franz Ruppert

Psychologist. Pioneers research into the effects of traumatic events on bonding in family systems. He developed several models about trauma. Recommended: *Symbiosis & Autonomy* (2012).

About the author: Jan Jacob Stam

Jan Jacob Stam was born in 1954, in Groningen, the Netherlands, the youngest child of a doctor's family. His mother's studies were cut short by the Second World War and his father became a radiotherapist, did a PHD on larynx cancer and became a Professor of Radiotherapy.

Jan Jacob grew up in the calmness of the post war years and, caught up in the emerging awareness of the environmental movement, he went to Amsterdam to study biology. After graduating, he moved with his girlfriend Bibi, later to become his wife, to the countryside in Groningen where they both became teachers.

Jan Jacob studied Education, worked as a teacher for ten years and then joined PTT-Telecom (at that time the Dutch national telephone company): first as a training consultant and then as a manager. He began to sense that organisations could function better and this resulted in him being invited to work in a consulting firm, where he later became a partner. Jan Jacob followed several NLP training courses given by Robert Dilts at the University of California at Santa Cruz. In 1995, in a personal crisis, someone introduced him to family constellations. From that moment on Jan Jacob and Bibi were fascinated by constellations and systemic work.

They began to study and train, attending many workshops; in 1998 they began to offer their own workshops and training courses in the Netherlands. In 2000 they founded the Dutch Bert Hellinger Institute and, a year later, the publishing house Het Noorderlicht.

Jan Jacob has facilitated constellations and trained practitioners in more than 25 countries, organised several international congresses and has authored two other books: Nederlandse Wind (Dutch Wind) in 2001 and Fields of Connection in 2007.

Jan Jacob has stayed in close contact with Bert Hellinger; while learning and growing with Bert and sharing his latest insights with him, an enduring friendship has developed.

Jan Jacob: *"Inside I feel like an explorer. I am excited by the constant stream of new revelations about how organisations, families and society work and I am deeply grateful that my learning continues".*

Bibi and Jan Jacob have two grown-up children.

About the editor: James G. Campbell

"Language is a wonder. Although we all might speak the same mother tongue, we do so each in our own unique way. Face to face, we have many tools to ensure we understand and are understood. But reading another's text presents us with the challenge of understanding the author's intentions rather than giving his or her words our own meaning, without those checks and balances. This is where the role of the editor comes in and it is a responsibility and challenge I enjoy. I see my job as doing as little as possible to a text while ensuring that the author's meaning comes through to as many readers as possible, whether they are reading in English as their mother tongue or their second, or even third, language. I'm constantly checking with myself (and, when necessary, with the author) that my opinions, beliefs and ideas are not slipping into the book unnoticed. At the same time I try to make the book easier to read by giving it flow and removing ambiguities. English versions of books tend to be the ones upon which further translations are based and this, too, informs and conditions how I edit. In the way that I work (I can't speak for other editors) there comes a point in the editing process when everything comes together in a kind of gestalt: the book emerges out of the letters, spaces, words and sentences, I can enjoy and appreciate it as a whole... and I know, then, we are almost home.

I was born in London in 1950 of Scottish parents and now live in an intentional community, in Eindhoven, the Netherlands, with my wife and 6-year-old daughter. I grew up playing football, mountain-biking and reading poetry. Football is now limited to watching Manchester United, the Netherlands has no mountains, but the joy, inspiration and support I find in poetry increases with each passing year.

I first experienced systemic work, in the form of constellations, around 1998, and in the ensuing 15 years or so I have followed many training courses and workshops, especially with Judith Hemming and Jan Jacob Stam. I've been working as a general (English Language) editor for about 10 years. My earlier activities include studying for a BSc in Chinese Medicine and many years of global sales management roles. My life always feels lighter in those moments when I feel here and true contact can occur."

James G. Campbell

About the translator: Dymphie Kies

Dymphie Kies has worked for several educational institutions and consulting companies. In 2004 she became an independent consultant. In an authentic and inspiring way she helps people to work in good health and with pleasure. Using her systemic perspective she brings people into contact with their talents, their possibilities and themselves. Dymphie regularly gives presentations about systemic phenomenological work and co-organises seminars about systemic work in organisations. She has co-written several articles and books on the subject. She has also been a part of the international project, SISC, an international research programme into the effects of constellations on illness and symptoms.

As the oldest daughter of a father with a wartime past, she has constantly been searching for greater depth and grounding in her life. In 2000 she came into contact with family constellations (as practised by Bert Hellinger). From that moment on she followed several training courses in family and organisational constellations and took part in international workshops.

She lives in Veenendaal, the Netherlands, with her partner and has two grown-up children.

About the Dutch Bert Hellinger Institute

The Bert Hellinger Institute the Netherlands (BHIN) was founded by Jan Jacob Stam and Bibi Schreuder in 2000 and since 2015, Barbara Hoogenboom is co-owner.

Bert Hellinger encouraged Jan Jacob to take this step and allowed him to use his name. To this day, we are in regular contact and exchange with Bert Hellinger, now 91 years old.

What characterizes BHIN is:

- On the one hand, the loyalty to the foundation of the systemic phenomenological work the way Bert Hellinger discovered and described it. Working with the consciences, the principles (workings) and the patterns that arise;

- On the other hand, the continuing, phenomenological, openness to what wants to develop and reveal itself. This means for example, that we look at this work and the role of facilitator in constellations in a different way than in 2000. And that we have said our farewell to habits and interventions that were previously customary.

We can imagine, and even encourage the participants in our courses, to incorporate systemic work in their 'own toolkit' with their other 'tools'. That they develop their own style and mix. But with the implicit assumption that people are clear in their communication about their mixture.

This is only possible, if at BHIN we stay, as purely and precisely as possible, close to the foundations or the phenomenological work. That is what we enjoy most, and with a lot of love. Ánd that is what we want people to recognise us for, both meanings of the word, in the outside world.

More information and contact:
info@hellingerinstituut.nl
www.hellingerinstituut.nl

About Systemic Books

Systemic Books is an international independent Publishing House focused on creating high quality content selected from the broad range of books available. The books range from classic to cutting edge work with new adaptations of the systemic school of thought and working. This way, Systemic Books aims to answer to the different levels of knowledge people have or need on systemic work.

Systemic Books wass founded in joint energy by Siets Bakker and Barbara Piper in 2016. When they met in 2015, their knowledge of and interest in the systemic perspective and their shared love for books, planted the seed for Systemic Books. This initiative combines their knowledge in the publishing world and efforts to make systemic work available to a global audience. We translate, edit and publish books. Great books about the systemic school of thought. We make use of all modern possibilities in publishing and printing to make these books available all over the world.

More information and contact:
contact@systemicbooks.com
www.systemicbooks.com

www.ingramcontent.com/pod-product-compliance
Lightning Source LLC
Chambersburg PA
CBHW071549200326
41519CB00021BB/6666